# Introducing Joseph Crawhall

Jo Meacock

**The Burrell**
COLLECTION

First published in 2022 by Glasgow Museums Publishing.
Text © Culture and Sport Glasgow (Museums) 2022.
Images © CSG CIC Glasgow Museums Collection, unless otherwise acknowledged.

ISBN 978-1-908638-37-3




Written by Dr Jo Meacock
Edited by Kim Teo
Designed by John Westwell and Jacqui Duffus
Photography by Maureen Kinnear and Iona Shepherd
Images supplied by Glasgow Museums Photo Library
www.csgimages.org.uk
www.glasgowmuseums.com

Front cover image: detail from *The Aviary, Clifton*, 1888, 35.77
Back cover image: *Girl on a Bicycle*, about 1896, 35.124

## Acknowledgements

All efforts have been made to trace copyright holders, but if any omissions have been made inadvertently, please contact the publishers. We are very grateful to the following for permission to reproduce images: The Art Institute of Chicago: p. 27, *Ballet at the Paris Opera*; National Galleries of Scotland: p. 10, *Joseph Crawhall*, p. 29, Crawhall in Morocco; SMO Stephen: p. 49, Constance and Marion Burrell; Tate: p. 29, Crawhall hunting near Tangier, Photo © Tate.

Printed in Scotland by J Thomson Colour Printers, Glasgow
Cover printed on 350gsm Galerie Satin; text printed on 150gsm Galerie Satin

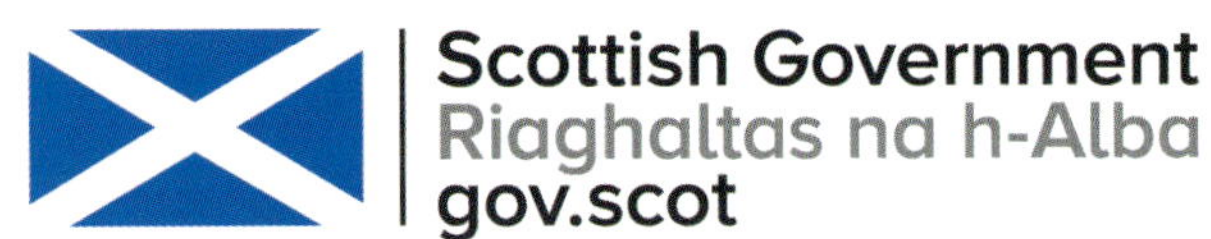


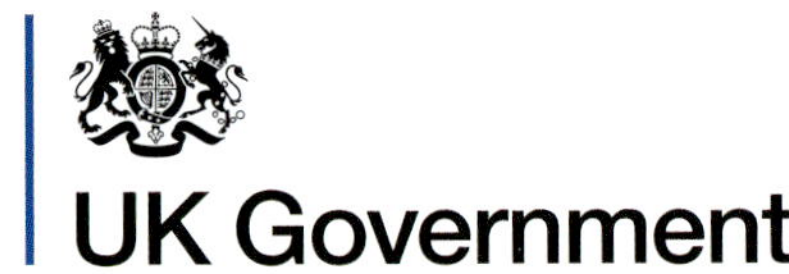

# Contents

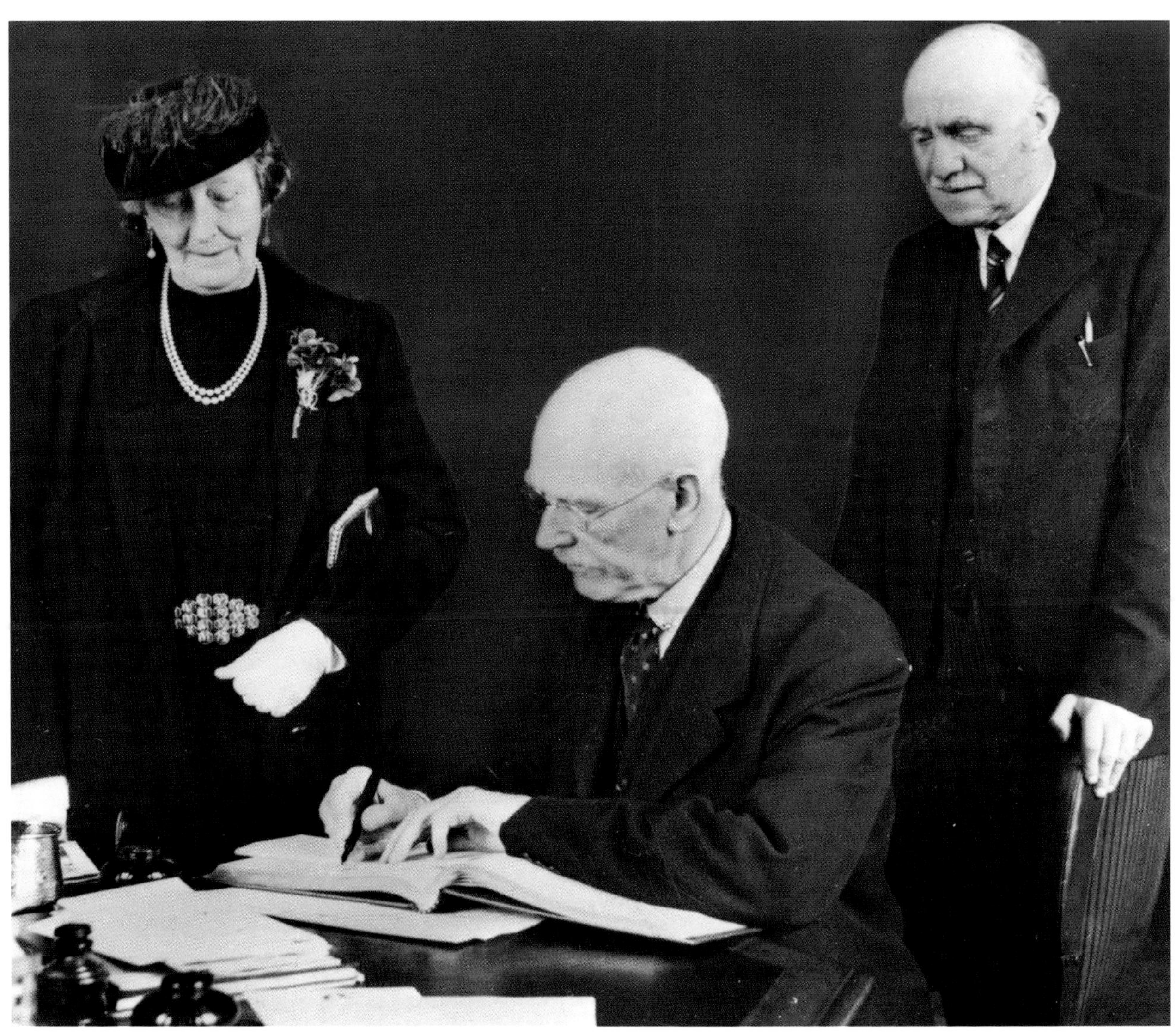

Sir William Burrell (seated), Constance, Lady Burrell and Lord Provost James Welsh at the City Chambers, Glasgow, 1944, on the occasion of Sir William receiving the Freedom of the City of Glasgow. Glasgow Museums Archive, GMA.2013.1.1.470.

# The Burrell Collection: The Gift of Sir William and Constance, Lady Burrell

The Burrell Collection comprises over 9,000 objects gifted to the city of Glasgow by Sir William Burrell (1861–1958) and his wife Constance, Lady Burrell (1875–1961). The main gift, of around 6,000 objects, was in 1944, but Burrell continued to add to it until his death, and the Collection has been further augmented with funds gifted by Burrell and administered by the Burrell Trustees.

Sir William made his fortune in shipping at a time when Glasgow was second city of the Empire. Collecting was a lifelong passion, and his treasures adorned his various homes: archive photographs show tapestries, sculpture, paintings and furniture in his house in Great Western Terrace, Glasgow. These, and also ceramics, stained glass, arms and armour and textiles, were displayed at Hutton Castle, his home in the Scottish Borders.

A sophisticated collector with a discerning eye, Burrell appreciated fine craftsmanship and meticulous attention to detail. From tapestries to sculpture, nineteenth-century French art to Chinese bronzes, medieval stained glass to Islamic carpets, the breadth and quality of his collection demonstrate his wide-ranging embrace of different cultures and art forms. Sir William also gave money for a new building to house his collection, and it is now displayed in a purpose-built museum in the centre of Pollok Country Park,

on the south side of Glasgow. The park was gifted to the city in 1967 by Mrs Anne Maxwell Macdonald (1906–2011), and a competition, sponsored by the Royal Institute of British Architects, was held to design a suitable building within it to house the Collection. The winners of the competition, architects Barry Gasson, John Meunier and Brit Andresen, came up with a building which not only displays the Collection to advantage, but is also in harmony with the surrounding parkland. The building opened in 1983, but through the decades the Scottish weather took its toll and in 2016 the Category-A listed building closed for an ambitious programme of refurbishment, redisplay and reinterpretation.

This series is designed to introduce different parts of the Collection. Written by subject specialists, each book gives an insight into the Burrell's treasures. We, the Trustees of The Burrell Collection, are delighted to see the amount of new research that has been carried out on the objects in the collection, and hope that visitors will continue to enjoy Sir William and Constance, Lady Burrell's gift for many generations to come.

Professor Frances Fowle
Senior Trustee, Sir William Burrell's Trust

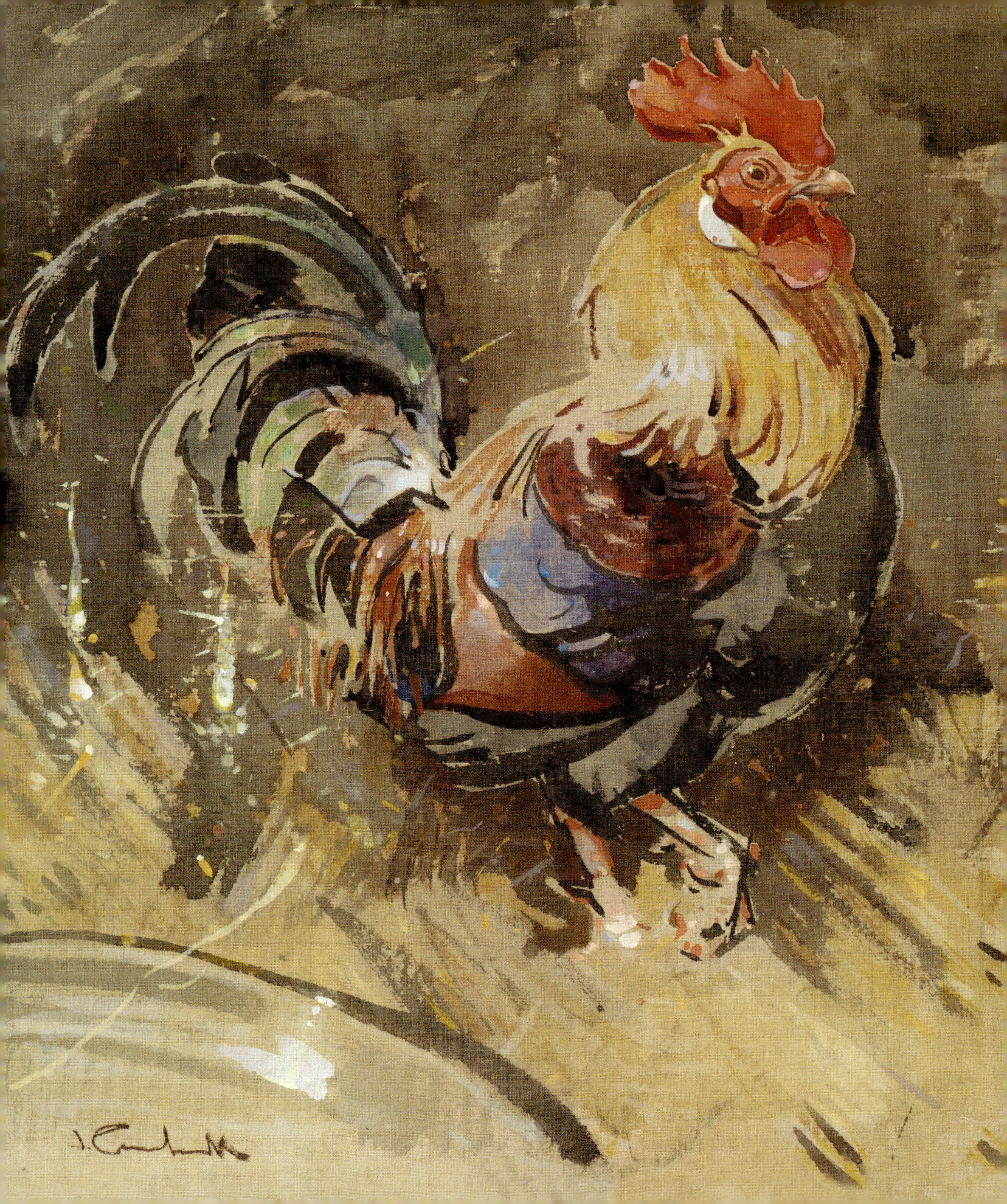

# Introduction

Joseph Crawhall (1861–1913) was a remarkable and innovative watercolourist, who made extraordinary studies of animals and birds. These were sensitively observed and elegantly drawn with an economy of line and vibrancy of colour, notable for their decorative balance and intrinsic humour. He was held up by his peers as a genius.

William Burrell began to collect Crawhall's paintings and drawings in the mid 1880s after seeing examples in exhibitions of the Glasgow Institute of the Fine Arts and the Scottish Society of Painters in Watercolour. Encouraged by Glasgow art dealer Alexander Reid (1854–1928), he developed an obsession for Crawhall's work. If he were offered an artwork by another artist, for example the renowned French Impressionist painter Edgar Degas (1834–1917), he would think long and hard about whether to buy it, but, according to one contemporary, 'if you offered him a Crawhall he would succumb at once.' On 13 April 1894 Burrell was honoured to be the only non-artist invited to a dinner party to celebrate Crawhall's inaugural exhibition at the new St Vincent Street premises of La Société des Beaux-Arts, Reid's gallery, an exhibition to which Burrell was a key lender and from which he bought several works.

Crawhall's output was irregular and his perfectionism led him to destroy many drawings, resulting in a very limited supply of works being available on the market. Burrell snatched up as many as he could, frustrating fellow collectors. He kept his eye on prized works in rival collections, buying them at the first opportunity. Reid complained that Burrell had too many Crawhalls and would not sell them on.

Burrell's single-minded collecting of Crawhall artworks was unique and spanned more than 60 years. Varied in subject matter, style, medium and date, the works he purchased give a comprehensive picture of Crawhall's talents and development as an artist, making it an invaluable collection for the study and understanding of the artist's practice. Burrell gifted three Crawhalls to the City of Glasgow in 1925 and 126 in 1944 (part of his and Lady Burrell's wider gift to the city), adding a further three in 1949 and two in 1952. In addition, Burrell's library was transferred from Hutton Castle to Glasgow in 1962; it included editions of Crawhall's father's illustrated publications, many of which contained pictorial contributions by Crawhall.  In 1968 the Burrell Trustees purchased 10 childhood drawings by Crawhall for the collection. Today the Burrell Collection holds the largest and most significant collection of Crawhall artworks in the world.

Opposite: *The Minorca Cock,* about 1903–08
Watercolour and bodycolour on linen
40.6 x 36.2 cm
35.157

This watercolour demonstrates Crawhall's brilliance in distilling the essence of a bird's character with minimal means and his natural feeling for colour and design.

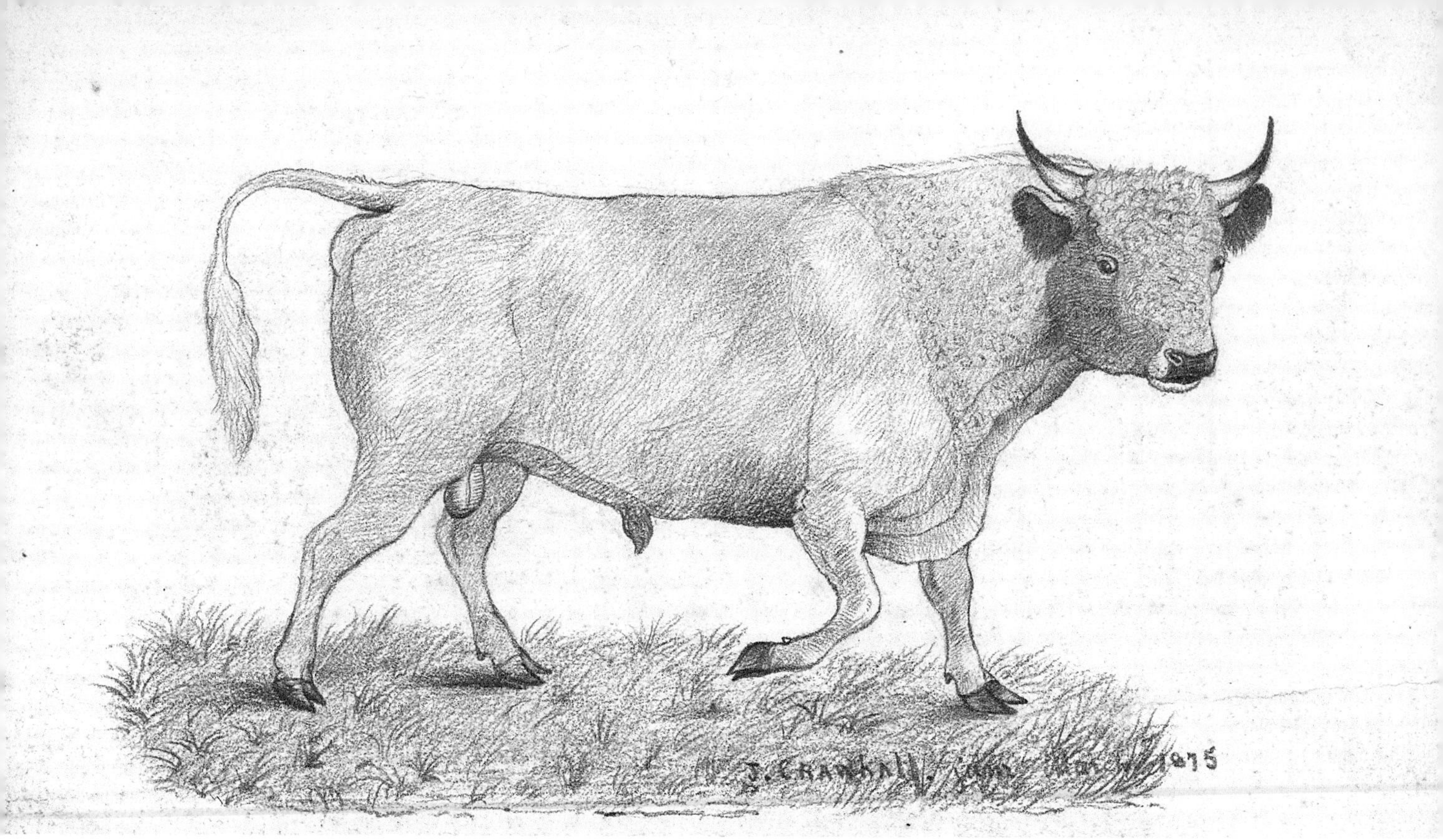

Above: ***The Bull,*** March 1875
Conte and graphite pencil on paper
13 x 22.9 cm
35.662

Made when Crawhall was 13 years old, this drawing of a bull
was copied from Thomas Bewick's famous wood engraving
*The Chillingham Bull* (1789). As a boy Crawhall often found
inspiration in the illustrations of Bewick, who had been a
friend of his grandfather.

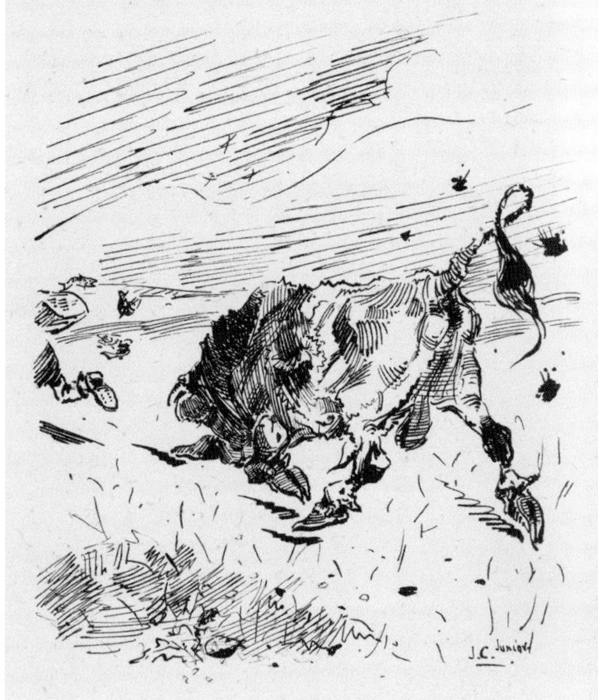


Left: Crawhall's rapidly maturing skills as an artist are evident
in this comic drawing of a fisherman fleeing a charging bull.
It shows first-hand observation, dexterity in capturing
character and movement, a cleverly selected compositional
angle and a developing sense of humour. Joseph Crawhall
illustration in *The Compleatest Angling Booke that euer was
writ*, by Joseph Crawhall snr, 1881. Glasgow Museums
Archive, GMA.2013.1.6.854.

# Crawhall's Early Years

Born on 20 August 1861 in the historic market town of Morpeth, near Newcastle, Northumberland. Crawhall was the son of a Scottish mother, Margaret Boyd (1833–1928), and an English father, Joseph Crawhall (1821–96), a prosperous ropemaker. The family was artistic. His grandfather Joseph Crawhall (1793–1853) had been an amateur watercolourist and had helped found the Northumberland Institution for the Promotion of Fine Arts in the North of England. Crawhall's father, a founder member of the Arts Association of Newcastle, was also a skilful amateur illustrator, his drawings notable for their observational wit. It was a happy and supportive environment in which Crawhall's artistic ability was recognized and encouraged.

Crawhall would apparently spend hours as a child lying in the fields watching the local livestock and wildlife. Many of his early drawings were copied from prints in his father's collection, for example, those of local wood engraver Thomas Bewick (1753–1828). From 1877 he attended King's College School in London, where he won prizes for his art in 1878 and 1879, and found that the humorous nature of his drawings had market appeal. From 1878 he showed his animal pictures at the biennial exhibitions of the Arts Association of Newcastle and was encouraged by artist and family friend Charles Keene (1823–91) to submit works to the Royal Academy's annual exhibition in London.

Crawhall never had a formal art school education. A letter of 1880 suggests his father tried to persuade him to study fine art in Antwerp. In the autumn of 1882 he enrolled in the Paris studio of animal painter Aimé Morot (1850–1913), perhaps in acknowledgement of his lack of professional technical training.

However, Crawhall only stayed in Paris for a couple of months and preferred to wander the boulevards and markets rather than attend the atelier. According to the artist Archibald Standish Hartrick (1864–1950), who Crawhall met in the French capital, Crawhall completed only one drawing at this time – of a bull – although many other drawings were begun and destroyed. But his time was not wasted. Crawhall visited the city's famous art galleries and museums, where his favourite work was a self-portrait by French Realist painter Gustave Courbet (1819–77) in the Louvre, an unexpected choice for an artist who avoided portraiture. He would also have seen the works of the French Naturalists and Impressionists in dealers' galleries, such as Durand-Ruel & Cie.

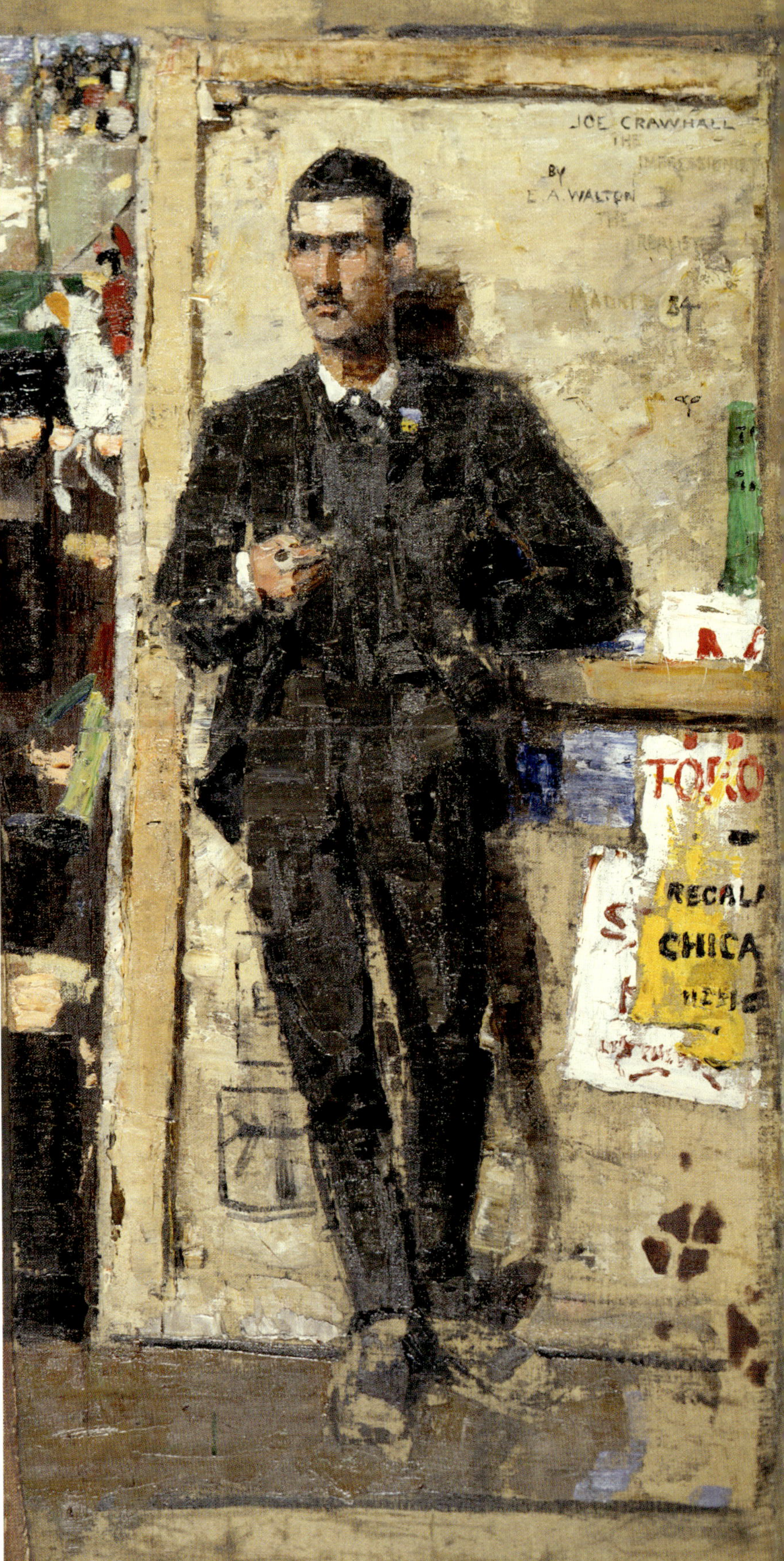

Left: The inscription on this portrait, 'JOE CRAWHALL THE IMPRESSIONIST BY E.A. WALTON THE REALIST', makes light of censure. Throughout the 1880s the Glasgow Boys were criticized for producing art that was insufficiently finished, considered too French and 'impressionist'. *Joseph Crawhall*, 1884, by Edward Arthur Walton, oil on canvas. National Galleries of Scotland, Edinburgh, PG 971, presented by Mrs EA Walton.

# Crawhall and the Glasgow Boys

Although based in Northumbria, Crawhall became closely connected with the Glasgow School of Painters, known today as the Glasgow Boys. He worked and exhibited with the group in the 1880s and shared many of their influences and aesthetic concerns. His work was promoted, as was theirs, by Glasgow art dealers Alexander Reid and William Bell Paterson (1859–1952), brother of Glasgow Boy James Paterson (1854–1932). Crawhall was a bit of an outsider, quiet and reserved by nature, known by his friends as 'the Great Silence' and 'Creeps', and yet Glasgow Boy John Lavery (1856–1941) declared that it was to him that 'the Glasgow School owed its greatest distinction.'

Crawhall first met the Boys in the late 1870s through his sister Judith (1860–1935), who married the elder brother of Edward Arthur Walton (1860–1922). Crawhall joined the St Mungo Art Society, a sketching club in Glasgow, of which EA Walton, James Guthrie (1859–1930) and George Henry (1858–1943) were members. They enjoyed summer sketching holidays together: Rosneath at Gare Loch in 1879 and 1880; Brig o'Turk in the Trossachs in 1880 and 1881; Crowland in Lincolnshire in 1882; and Cockburnspath in the Scottish Borders in 1883 to 1885, where they were joined by a wider set of Glasgow artists. Influenced by the French Naturalist painter Jules Bastien-Lepage (1848–84), they immersed themselves in rural life.

Crawhall may have met up with other Glasgow Boys, including Lavery, Paterson and William Kennedy (1859–1918), while studying in Paris. They certainly got together in Glasgow, the Bath Street studio of William York Macgregor (1855–1923) becoming a regular meeting place for the group. Glasgow was an exciting place to be for a young artist. Its shipping, coal, iron and textile industries were thriving, and prosperity meant that there was a flourishing art market. Glasgow was well connected with Europe and there were opportunities to see new works by French Realist, Naturalist, Barbizon, Impressionist and Dutch Hague School painters for sale in the premises of dealers such as Reid, Craibe Angus & Son and Thomas Lawrie, at loan exhibitions at the Glasgow Institute of the Fine Arts and Corporation Galleries, and at the city's International Exhibitions of 1888 and 1901.

Crawhall was distinct from the Glasgow Boys in his focus on painting animals and birds, but he shared their interest in the everyday, feeling for colour and tonal values, decorative approach to compositional design and tendency to suggest rather than describe form. Like the Boys, he was influenced by contemporary Dutch and French art, by the colour harmonies of American artist and aesthete James McNeill Whistler (1832–1903) and by Japanese prints.

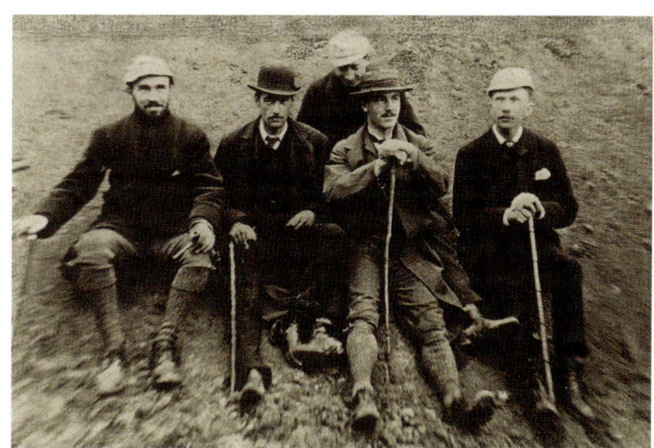

Crawhall often joined the Glasgow Boys on painting trips to rural Scottish locations. This 1883 photograph taken in Cockburnspath shows (left to right): EA Walton, Crawhall, George Walton (1867–1933), James Guthrie and James Whitelaw Hamilton (1860–1932). Photo: T & R Annan & Sons Ltd.

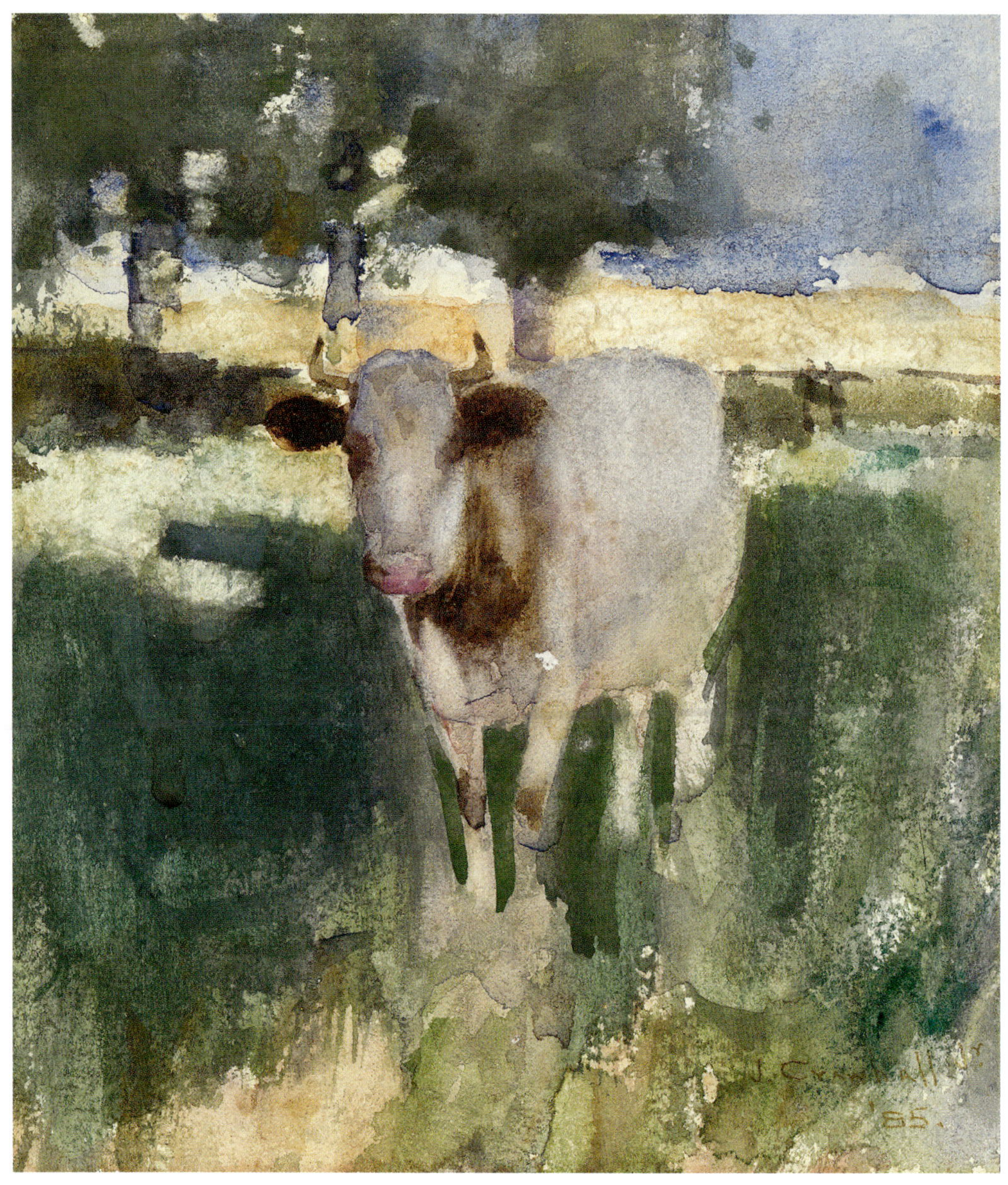

***Calf,*** 1885
Bodycolour and watercolour on paper
16.5 x 14 cm
35.90

Crawhall's works, like those of the Glasgow Boys, were a reaction against the sentimental narrative paintings and romantic literary landscapes that were so popular in the 1880s. This early watercolour, probably painted out of doors in Cockburnspath, shows Crawhall's interest in simple rural life. It is not descriptive or finished in any traditional sense, but gives the feel of a warm summer's day under the trees. In Cockburnspath in 1883–85, Crawhall had begun moving away from oils to painting in watercolour, inspired by Glasgow Boy Arthur Melville (1855–1904). Rather heavy-handed in places, this watercolour evidences his early experiments with the medium.

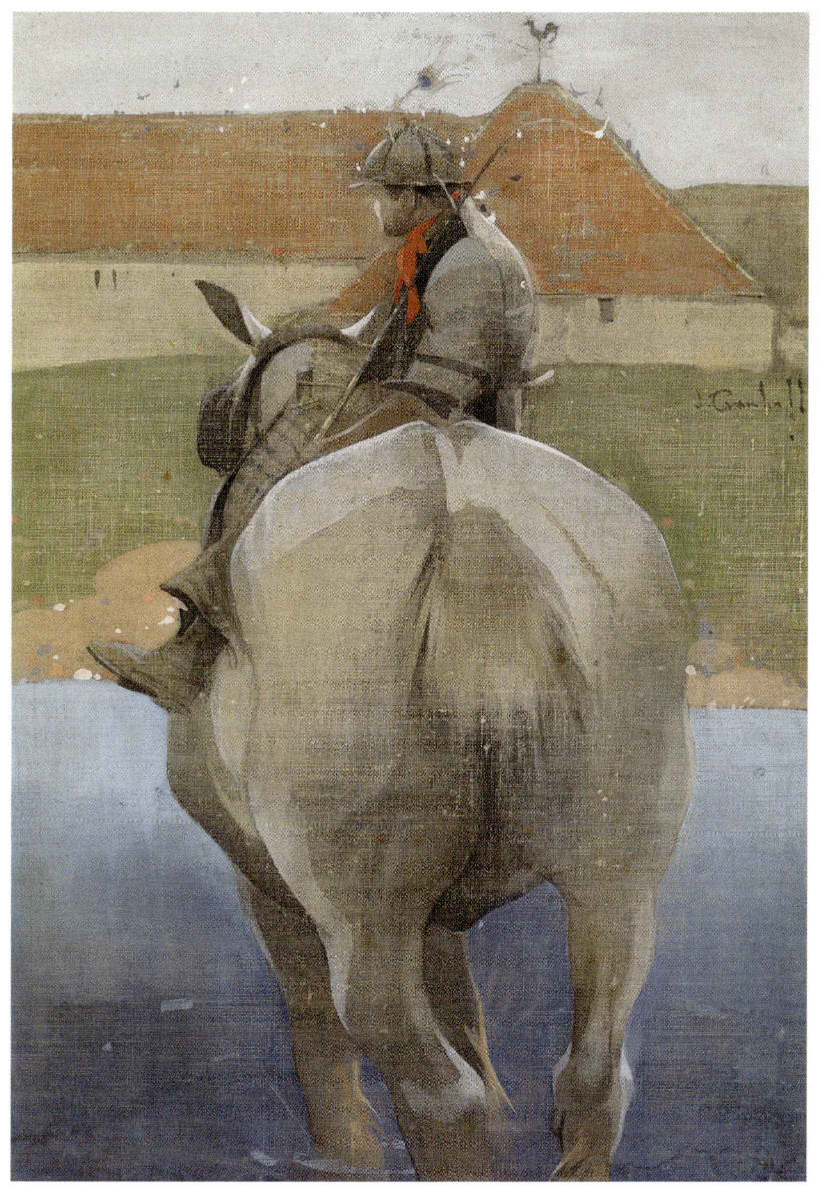

***The Farmer's Boy,*** 1895
Bodycolour on linen
30.5 x 20.4 cm
35.112

Crawhall continued to follow the original tenets of the Glasgow Boys into the 1890s. Here he not only chose a blatantly unheroic subject, a farm boy on a workhorse wearily returning from a day in the fields, but playfully focused on the horse's ample rump and docked tail. Typically well observed, the horse has its ears back listening to the boy. Despite the mundanity of the scene, the composition is innately decorative, the background simplified into a stylized flat pattern, the peacock feather in the boy's cap a nod towards Aestheticism. Burrell bought it, together with *The Chinese Goose* (p. 53), from WB Paterson on 22 March 1918 for a combined price of £750.

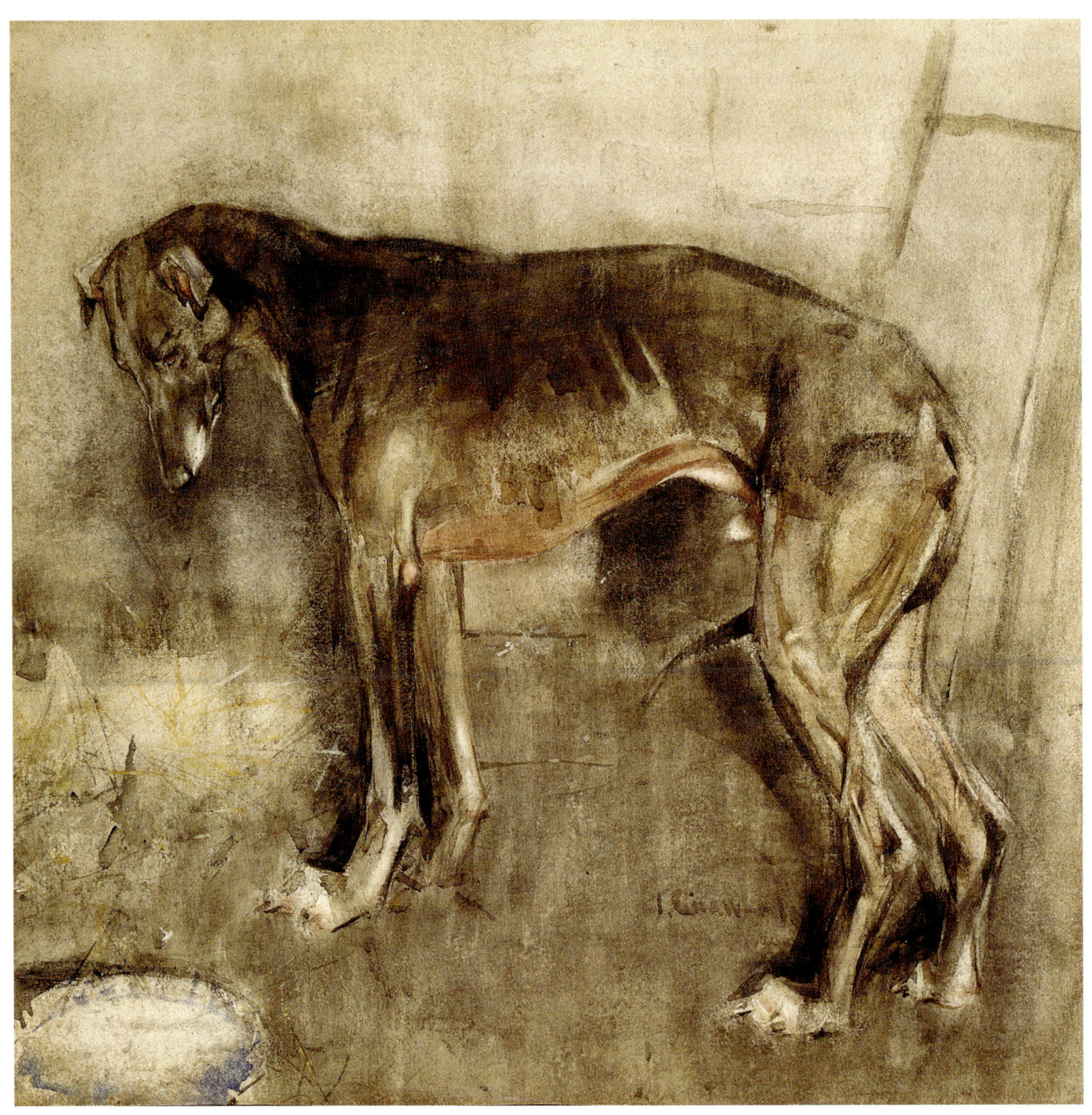

***The Greyhound,*** about 1884
Watercolour on paper
38.8 x 38.5 cm
35.130

This sensitively observed watercolour of a greyhound in a barn, tail between its legs, gazing mournfully at its empty bowl, is composed with a Whistlerian balance and elegance. Could the blue-and-white earthenware dish be a wry nod to the more precious examples of Chinese porcelain that the American artist carefully placed within his aesthetic arrangements? The muted tones and sombre mood may also reflect the influence of the Dutch Hague School of painters, sometimes known as the Grey School, whose paintings of nature and everyday life were popular with Scottish collectors like Burrell and much admired by the Glasgow Boys.

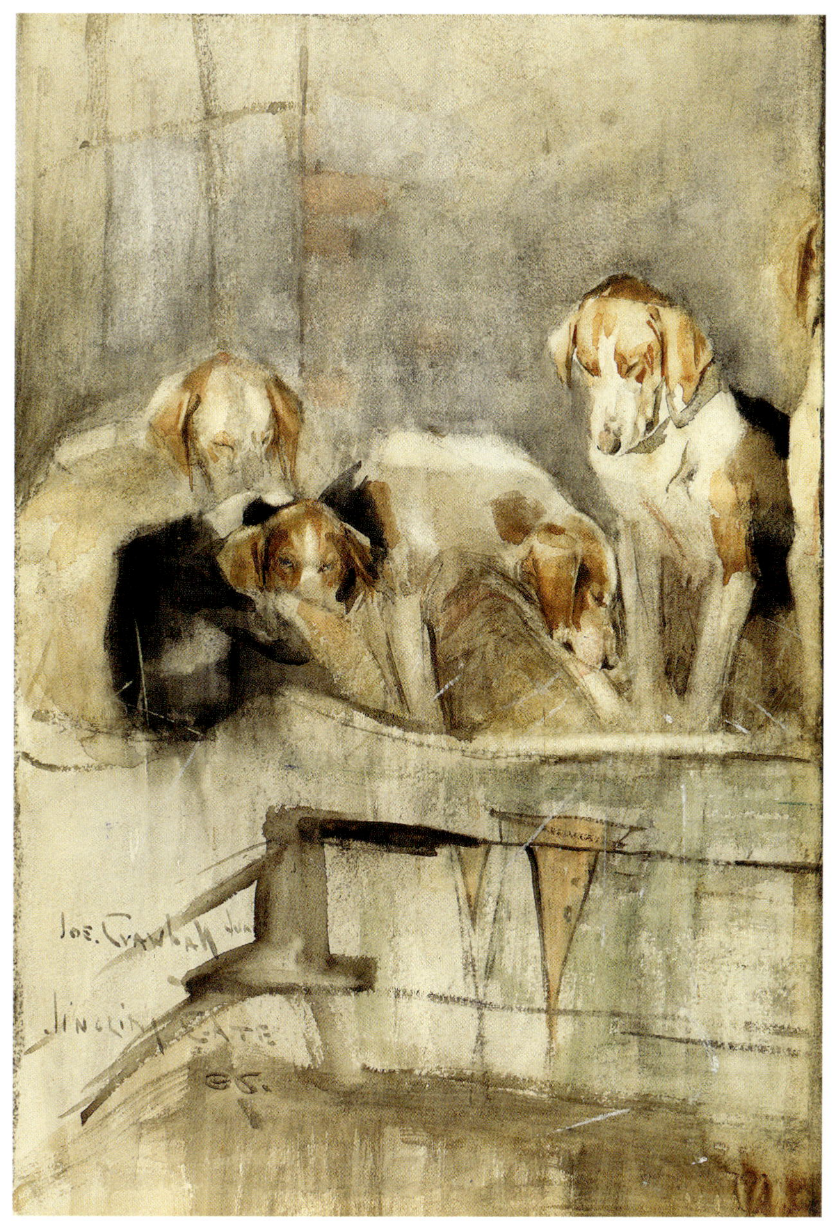

**Foxhounds – Jingling Gate,** 1885
Watercolour and bodycolour on paper
49.5 x 33 cm
35.119

Crawhall's ability to capture an animal's individuality, here the hounds of the Northumbrian Hunt, was praised by his Glasgow Boy friends. *In The Life* *of a Painter*, Lavery wrote of Crawhall: 'In a few lines he could sketch an animal, making it more recognizable than the most candid camera could do – and this from memory. If he did a pack of hounds the huntsman would be able to recognize every single one, even when it was only indicated in half a dozen marks on the linen or paper he happened to be working on.'

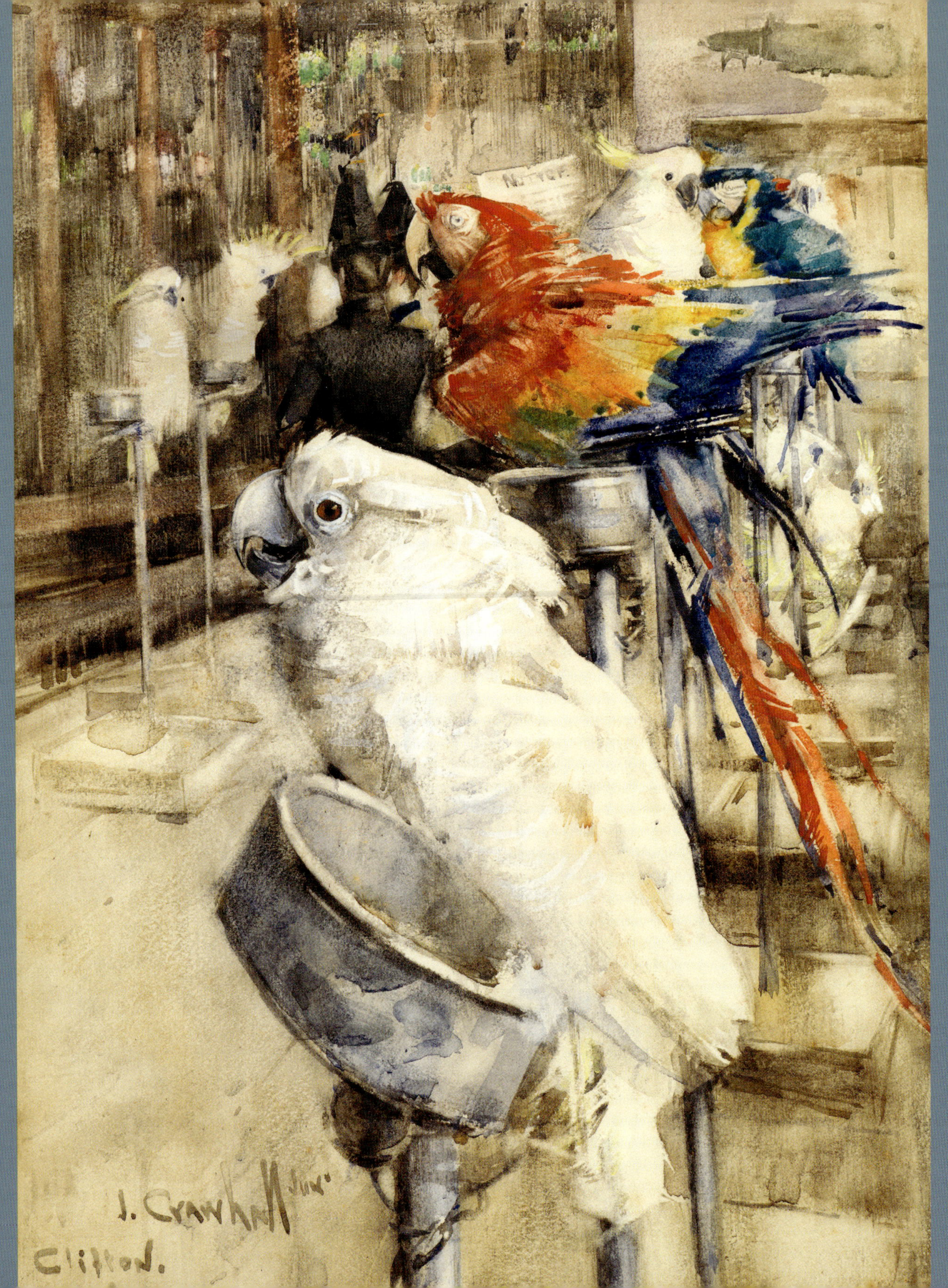

J. Crawhall jun.
Clifton.

# Artwork in Focus

*The Aviary, Clifton,* 1888
Watercolour and bodycolour on paper
50.5 x 35.1 cm
35.77

Inspired by a trip to the new parrot and reptile house at Bristol Zoo in Clifton, when Crawhall was visiting his sister Judith and her family, this watercolour showcases Crawhall's skill in capturing the substance of a bird's individuality and character. His quick brushstrokes convey a sense of movement and vitality as the birds ruffle their plumage, shuffle on their perches, raise their crests and squawk in alarm.

In the background, Crawhall's sister and her friend, dressed in black, are completely outshone by the plumage of the macaws and cockatoos. A mynah bird appears to perch mischievously on one of their hats. Crawhall may have intended to satirize the contemporary fashion for women's hats to be adorned with feathers from exotic birds. The Society for the Protection of Birds was formed in 1889 in direct response to this cruel trade.

Although one of Crawhall's most decorative compositions, with its vibrant colour, lively brushwork and immediacy, this watercolour was actually rescued from the bin by WB Paterson. It made Crawhall's reputation internationally. Chosen for exhibition at the 1890 International Exhibition in Munich, it was awarded a second-class gold medal and went on to travel to Berlin, Barcelona and Vienna, and then St Louis, Chicago, Cincinatti, New York and Philadelphia, to critical acclaim. Burrell bought it from Paterson & Thomas in 1892. He lent it to Crawhall's first solo exhibition at Alexander Reid's gallery in Glasgow in April 1894.

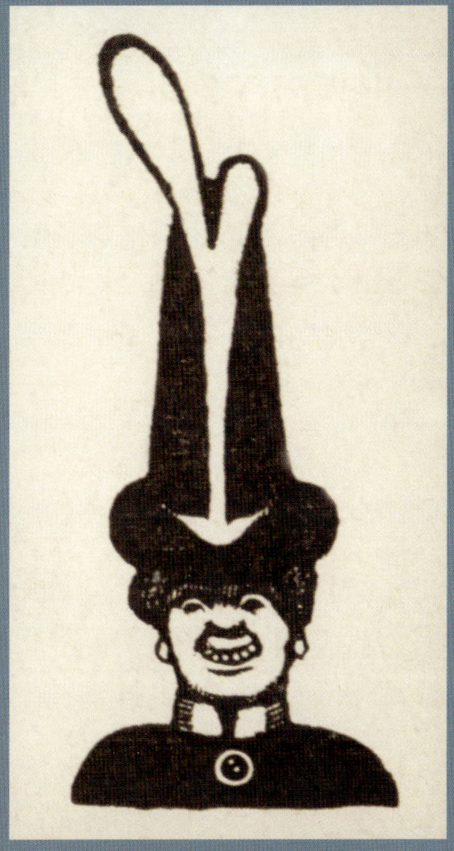

The year before Crawhall painted *The Aviary, Clifton*, his father had similarly mocked the fashion for feathered hats in a book of rhymes and quips: 'Now Babel's tower of gew-gaws skyward spring, / Alp upon Alp of feathers – flowers – furs.' Joseph Crawhall snr illustration in *A Jubilee Thought. Imagined and adorn'd by Joseph Crawhall*, 1887. Glasgow Museums Archive, GMA.2013.1.6.848.

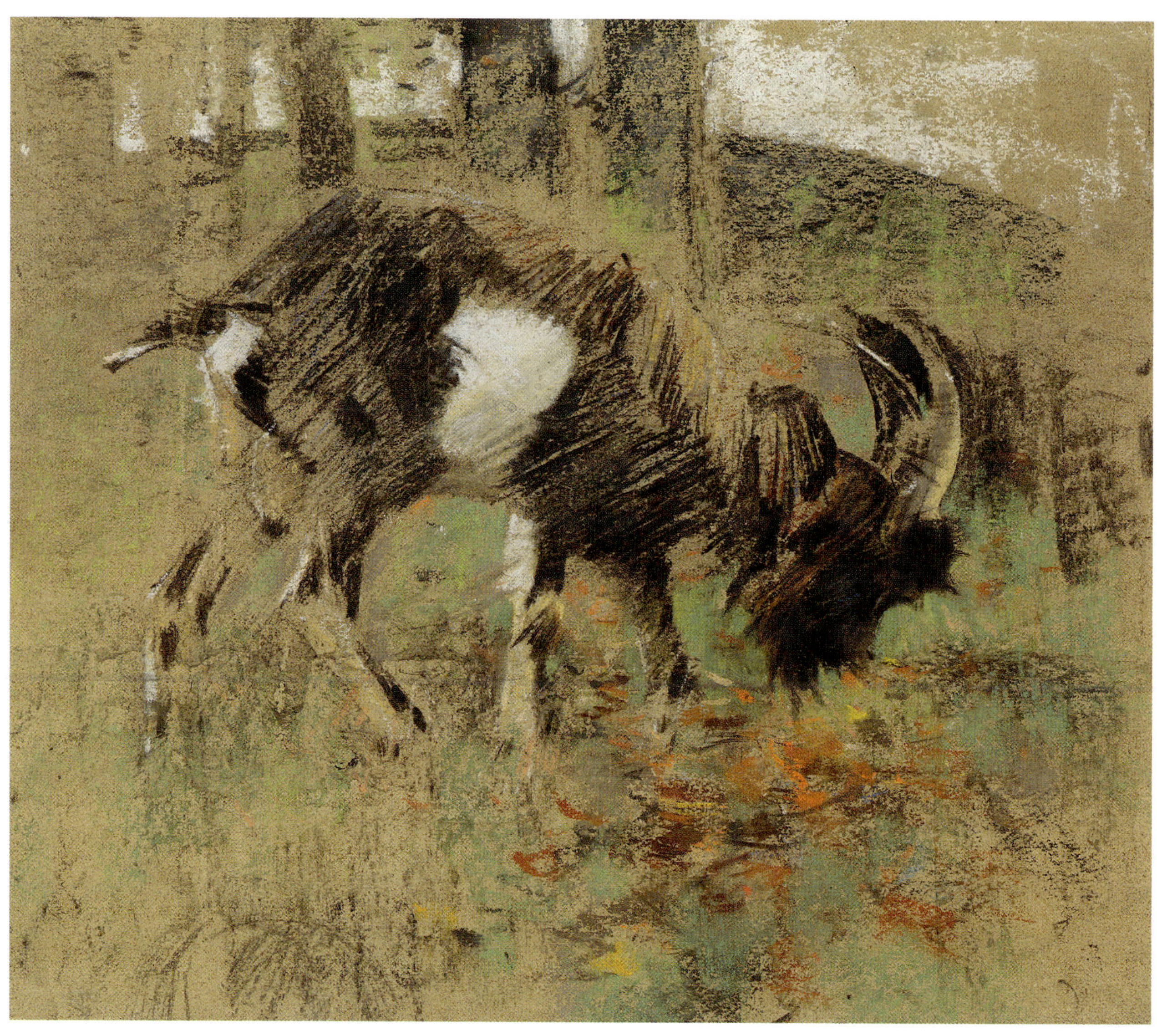

***The Goat,*** 1889
Pastel on paper
34.2 x 37.8 cm
35.126

In the late 1880s there was a revival of interest
in pastel and Crawhall and several other of the
Glasgow Boys began to explore the rich colour and
immediacy of the medium. This pastel of a belted
Galloway feral goat in an autumnal woodland was
probably drawn while Crawhall was visiting George
Henry and EA Hornel (1864–1933) in Kirkcudbright.
Hornel's friends teased him for his obsession with
goats, James Pittendrigh Macgillivray (1856–1938)
in 1888 composing the bawdy poem 'Hornel
Exultant to his Goat on the Galloway Hills'.
However, unlike Hornel, Crawhall was not interested
in any bovid symbolism or folklore, his was a
straightforward animal study and experimentation
with pastel mark making.

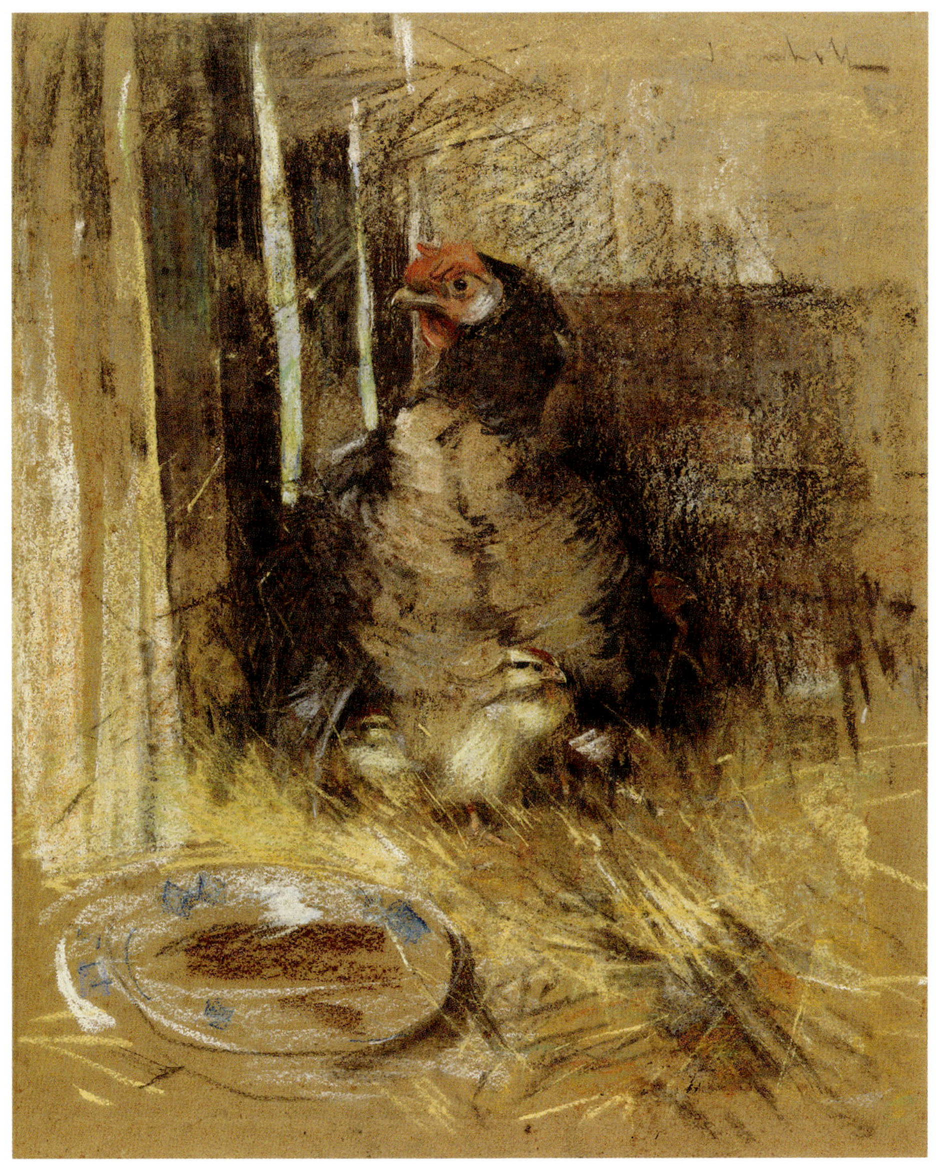

### *Hen and Chickens,* 1889

Pastel on paper
63.5 x 48.9 cm
35.133

Light falls through the slats of a henhouse on a proud mother with her hatchlings. Crawhall clearly enjoyed the play of light on straw in this dim interior. He smudged the pastel to suggest the blur of movement of chicks and wings, and the soft down of feathers.

His marks are various, creating sharp lines with the end of the crayon to indicate their scratchy bed of straw. The composition is carefully balanced, a delicate orchestration of primary colours. The brown paper lends a warm background tone.

To encourage pastellists, the Glasgow Boys persuaded the Glasgow Institute of the Fine Arts to hold an exhibition in the autumn of 1889 focusing on works on paper. Crawhall exhibited *Hen and Chickens*.

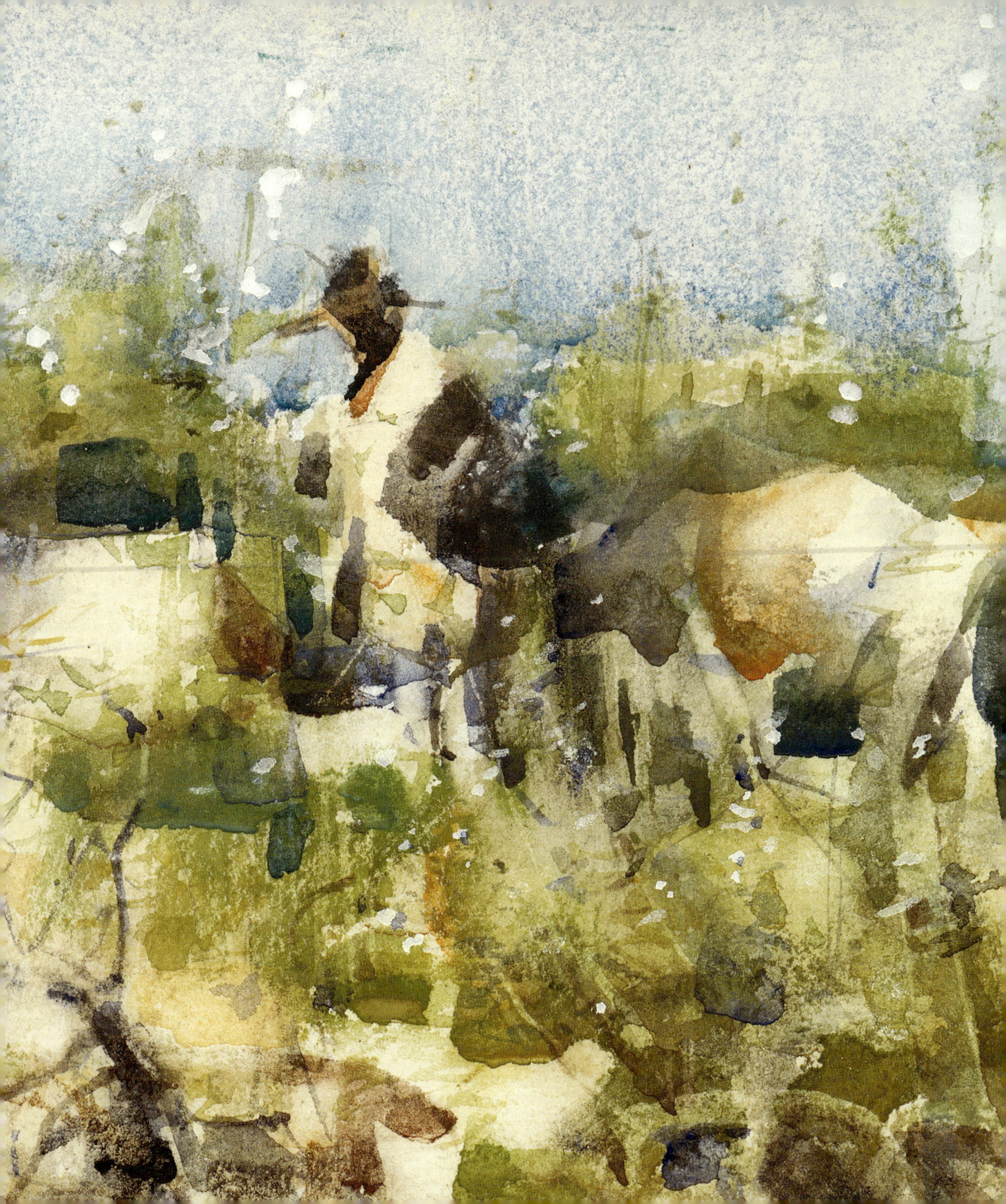

# Technique and Innovation

From a young age Crawhall developed an acute visual recall. His father taught him to closely observe nature and paint without correction from memory, a skill reinforced in Paris by Morot. He eliminated extraneous detail and focused on the key defining characteristics of his subject, giving his works a tremendous immediacy.

Crawhall was different from the majority of the Glasgow Boys, with the exception of Melville, in concentrating on the medium of watercolour. Its fluidity and speed suited him. Historically watercolour was considered an amateur or preparatory medium and had a lower status than oil. Watercolour paintings were given less prominence in exhibitions and fetched lower prices. The formation of the Scottish Society of Painters in Watercolour, in Glasgow in 1878, helped change perceptions; Crawhall was a member from 1887.

Crawhall used the medium in adventurous new ways. The artist Hartrick described Crawhall's unconventional technique. He would put a 'drawing under the tap with the water running, watching it till it came to the state he sought for; then, laying it flat, he would finish it with a few bold touches of sharp drawing or strong colour which brought out the character and life to perfection.' Sometimes he scratched into the wet paper, removing surface layers to create highlights.

The way he bled colours together and sponged out areas was close to Melville's experimental 'blottesque' technique. His works were criticized as eccentric and obscure, unfinished by academic standards.

In the late 1880s Crawhall began experimenting with painting on linen, first on the cover of a sketchbook and then later during a visit to his sister Judith in Bristol, using some brown holland from her sewing box. The fabric was a challenging support to work on because of its absorbency. Washes would sink into it and disappear. Colours merged in ways that were difficult to control. But Crawhall learnt to exploit its strengths. He explored different grades of cloth, fine and coarse, for texture. Increasingly he used bodycolour – watercolour mixed with a white pigment to create opacity – which sat on the surface of the fabric, giving intensity and helping define form. His works lost something of their spontaneity but gained in precision and detail.

At the time progressive artists, like Whistler and Degas, were influenced by the perceived startling originality of Japanese prints, with their different approach to perspective, unusual vantage points and decorative qualities. Crawhall too was inspired by their pictorial construction and design, and by the elongated format, elegant calligraphic lines and sense of proportion of Chinese silk paintings.

Opposite: Crawhall was innovative and experimental as a watercolourist, his mark making often independent of form. Here the horizontal swipes of paint and spattering of white bodycolour are decorative, not representational. Pigment spreads, runs, overlaps. *Goats on a Hillside, Tangier* (detail; see also p. 22).

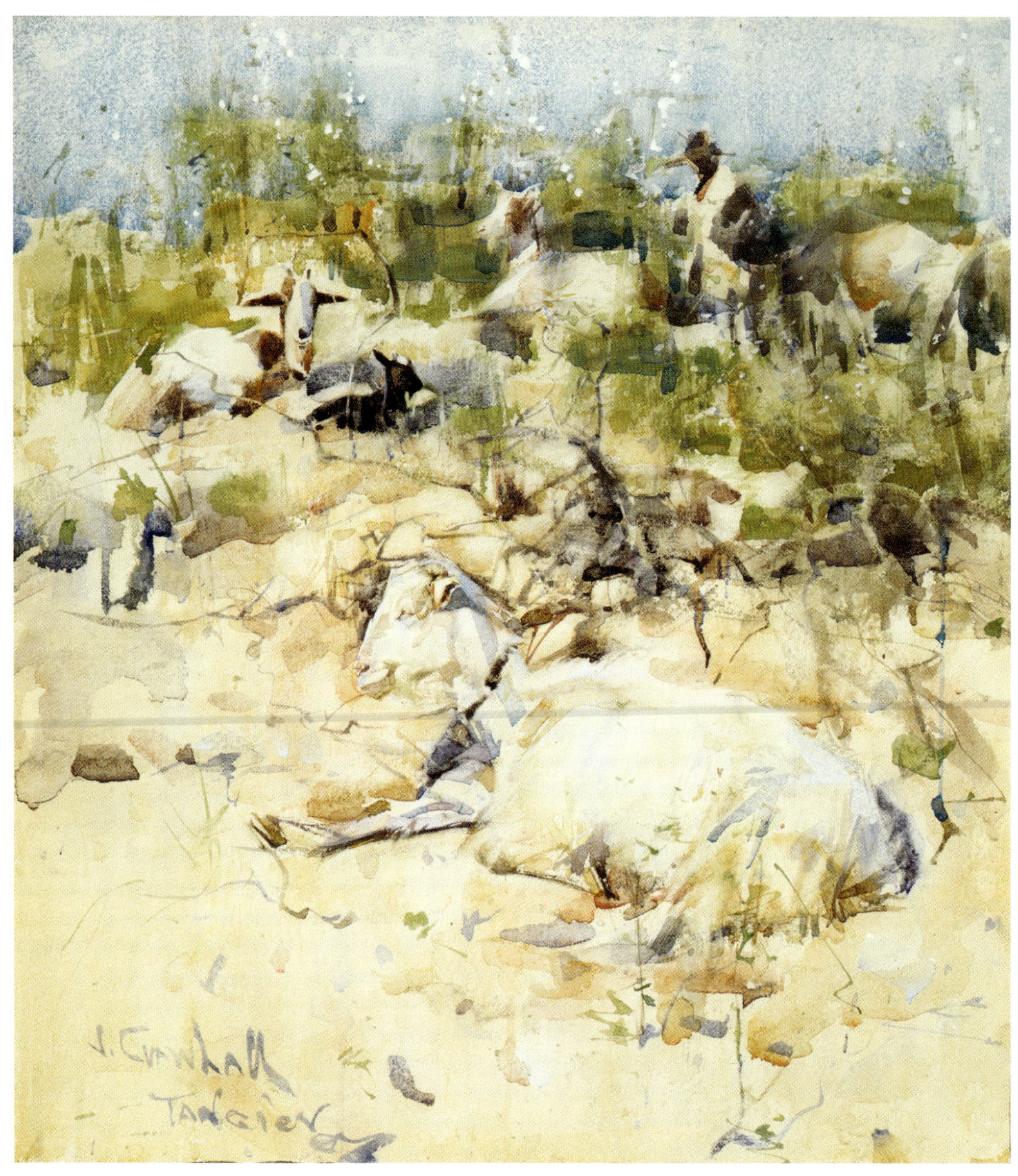

***Goats on a Hillside, Tangier,*** 1887
Watercolour and bodycolour on paper
38.8 x 33.7 cm
35.645

In this experimental composition, thin transparent
washes of watercolour have been allowed to run
together, creating a decorative, almost abstract
pattern. The goats appear to dissolve into the
landscape. Through the pale bleached colours and
prone forms of the herd, Crawhall suggests the
shimmering, energy-sapping noonday heat. The high
horizon line flattens the composition and locks the
goats into their sandy hillside habitat. Crawhall, with his
consummate sense of design, does not allow our eyes
to flounder over the disintegration of form, but anchors
our attention on a black kid beside its mother, realized
with the slightest of means but the greatest of skill.

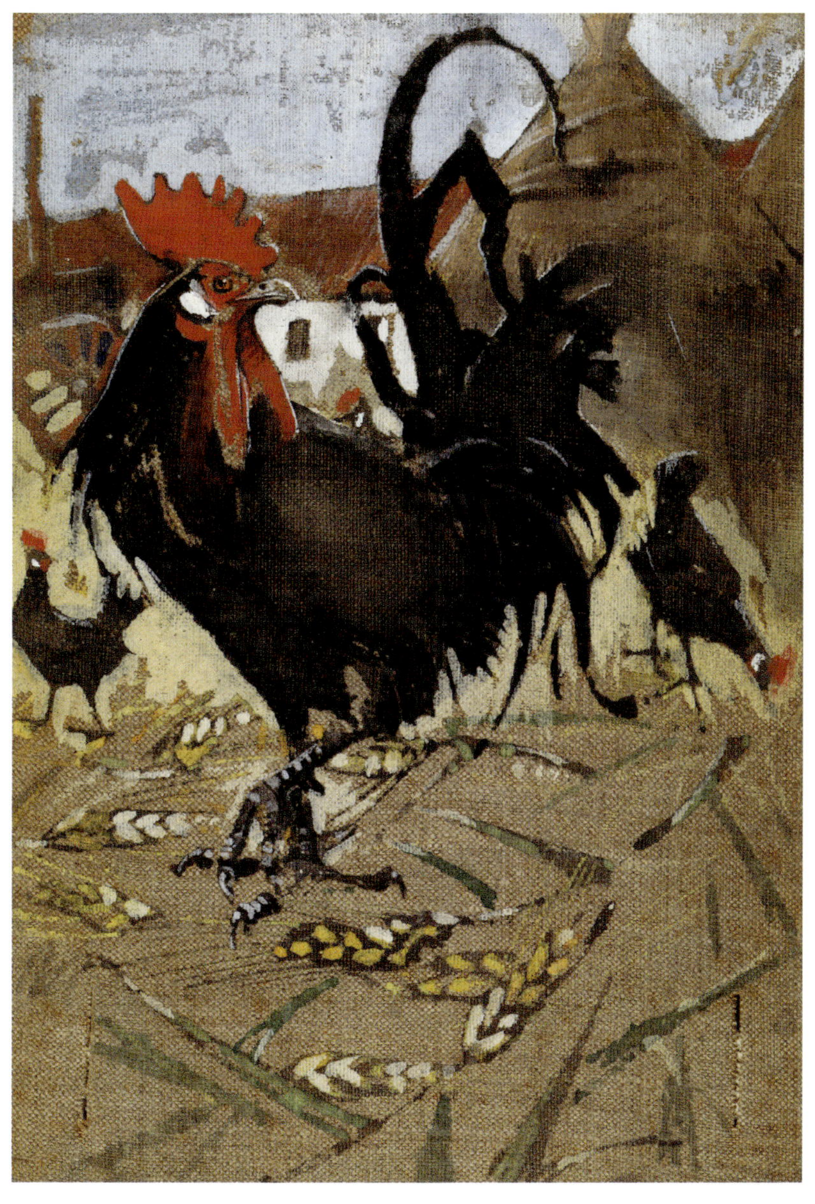

***Black Spanish Cock,*** 1888
Bodycolour on linen on board (sketchbook cover)
18.5 x 12.7 cm
35.83

Painted on the cover of a sketchbook – two binding slits are still visible near the lower corners – this picture for Newcastle artist William Henry Charlton (1846–1918) represents one of Crawhall's first works on linen. With its rather blocky use of colour, it perhaps lacks the pictorial sophistication of his later paintings on a finer grade of linen, but it shows Crawhall as a master of observation and design. The low viewpoint gives the strutting cockerel prominence and emphasizes its status within the brood. Crawhall perfectly captures the bird's swagger, its magnificent red comb and wattle, and its proudly held tail feathers. Its left leg is raised with as much elegance as a dressage-trained horse.

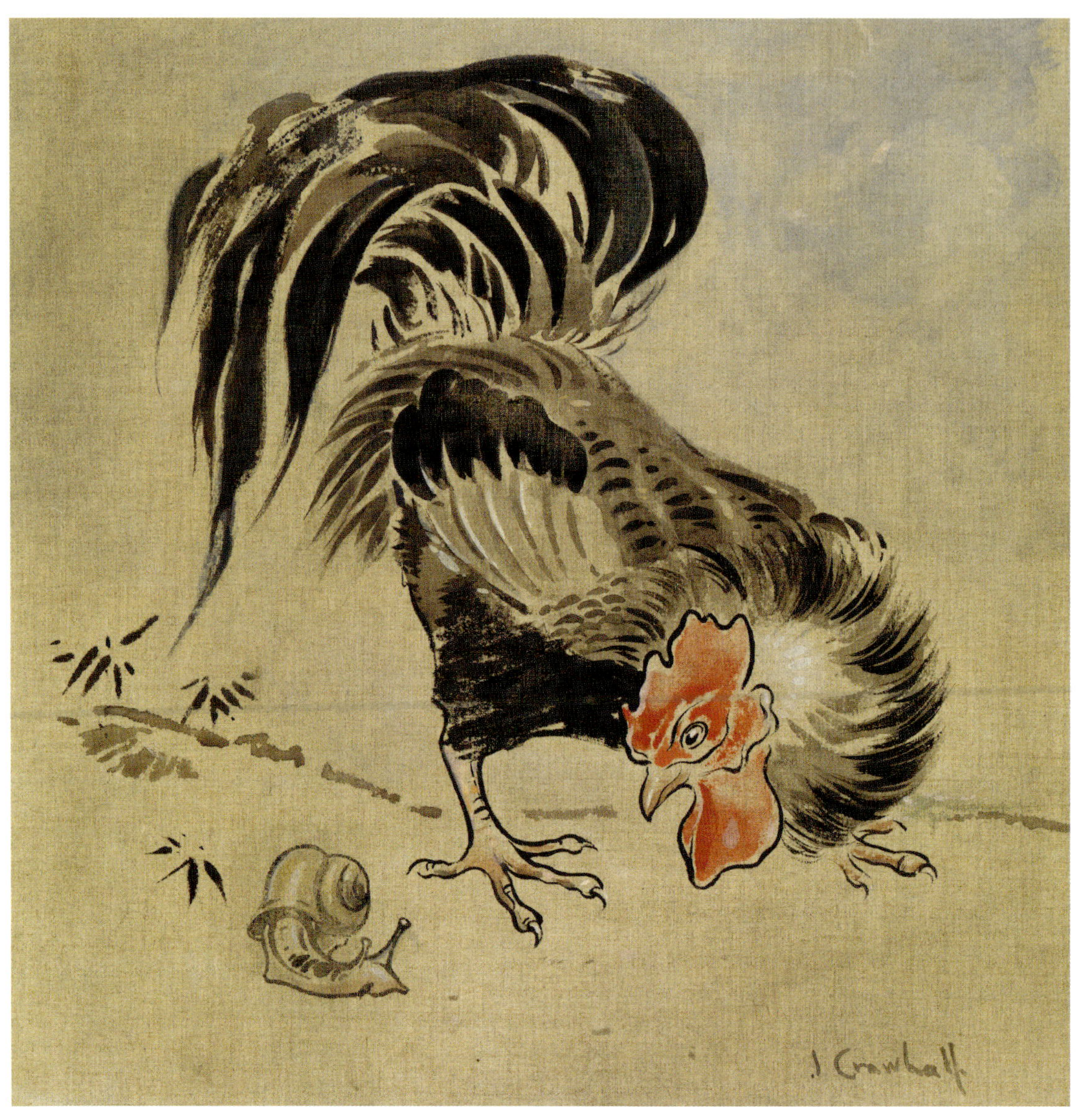


**_Spanish Cock and Snail,_** about 1894–99
Bodycolour on linen
31.8 x 30.5 cm
35.189

The poetic selection and isolation of the cockerel and snail against an undefined background, the simplification of colour and form and the almost calligraphic use of line in this painting all suggest a knowledge of East Asian art.

Crawhall had many opportunities to see Japanese prints, for instance in his father's collection and in the galleries of Glasgow dealers. In November 1889 Alexander Reid held an exhibition of Japanese woodcuts from the Parisian emporium of Siegfried Bing (1938–1905). Lavery recalled Crawhall's first purchase of a Japanese print, aged 20: 'He stood before it for a long time in silence, and then with great enthusiasm wishes to buy it.'

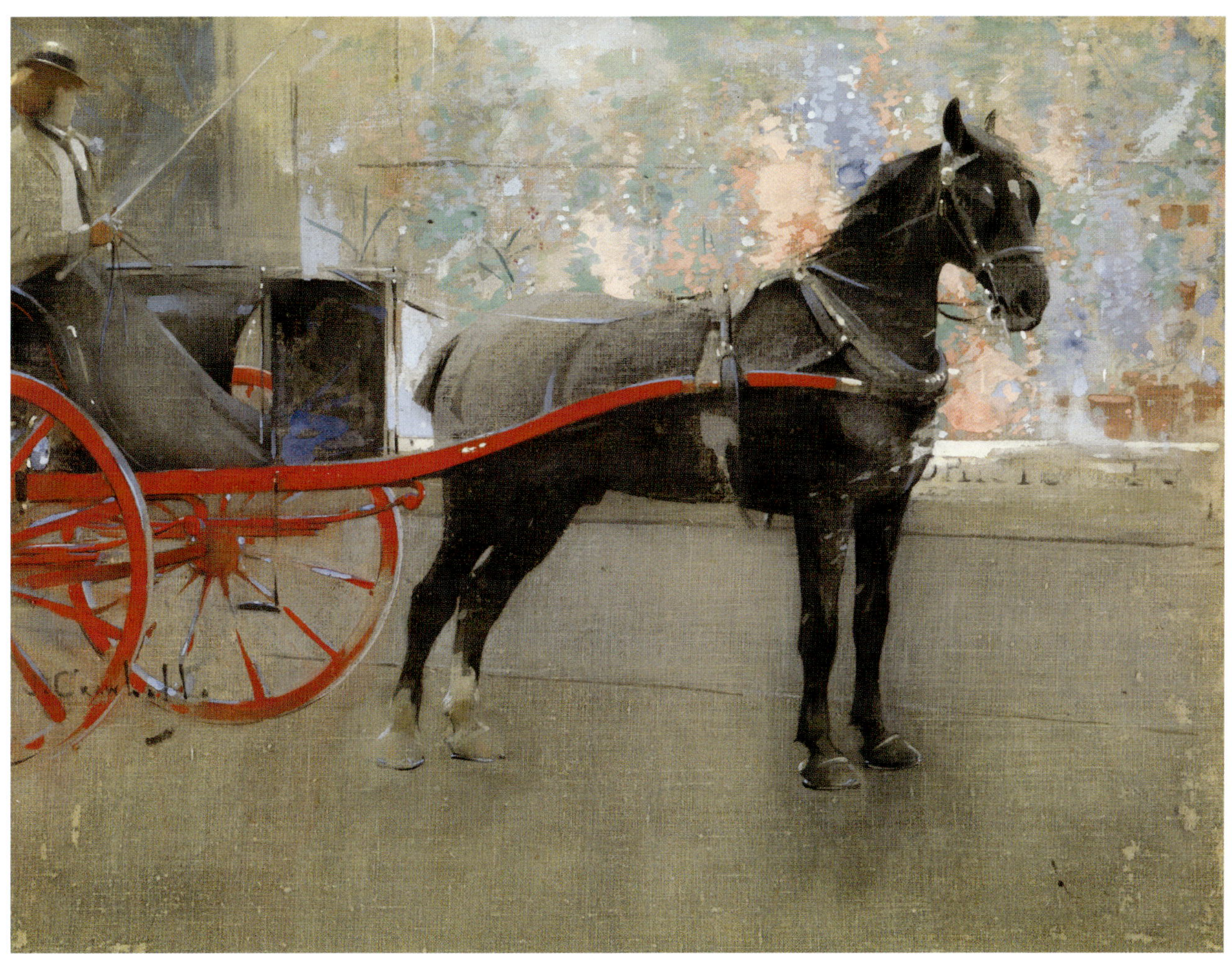



***The Flower Shop,*** about 1894–1900
Bodycolour on linen
34 x 40 cm
35.117

A woman pauses with her horse and carriage outside a flower shop with its colourful floral display. The red shaft of the carriage creates a striking contrast against the black flanks of the horse, elegantly posed in near-profile. This decorative composition clearly shows the influence of Japanese prints in its bold colour, strong lines, lack of pictorial depth and audacious cut-off on the left. It is also reminiscent of the work of French Impressionist Degas, whose paintings Crawhall could have seen in Reid's Glasgow gallery. Degas depicted modern urban life from unexpected angles, with daring cropping to disorientate and add a psychological aspect.

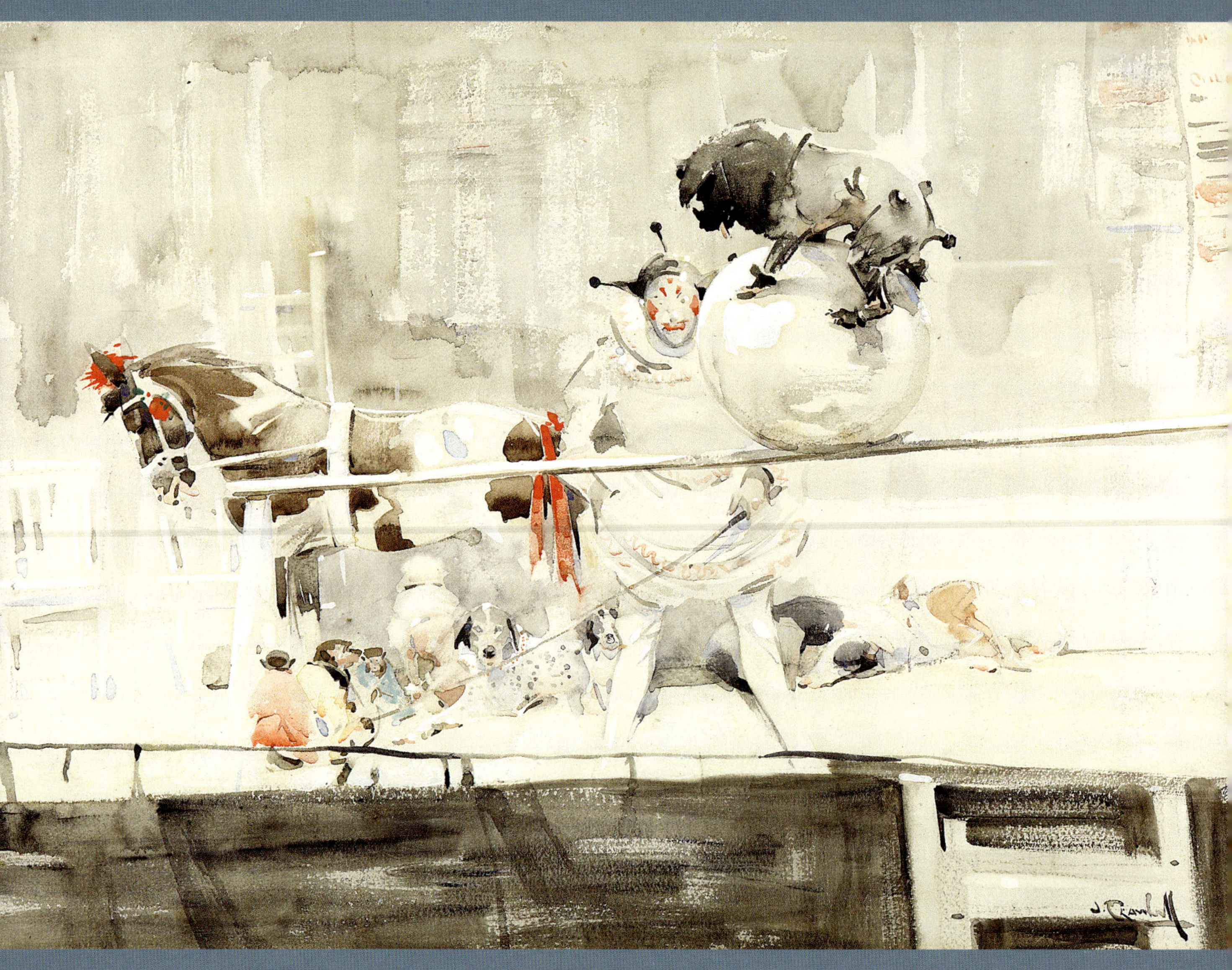

# Artwork in Focus

**_The Circus,_** 1893
Watercolour and bodycolour on paper
43.2 x 59.7 cm
35.99

Crawhall enjoyed unusual compositional formats. This picture is bisected by a horizontal pole, along which a circus dog, its tongue out in concentration, precariously makes its way balancing on top of a ball, watched by a sinister clown with a whip. In the background a skewbald horse, a poodle, dalmatians, hounds and monkeys in coloured jackets wait their turn to perform. Two chairs and a ladder suggest clowning acrobatics to come. However, there is little sense of fun or excitement. The muted colouring, conveying the glare of artificial light, adds to the sense of tension and unease. The edge of the ring shown in the foreground positions the viewer in the first row of the audience, where we feel the performing dog's anxiety. The format is reminiscent of Degas' views of the theatre or ballet where the stage is viewed from the vantage point of the boxes or stalls.

In 1927, Burrell was willing to pay £750 for this work, demonstrating how highly he valued it – Paisley thread manufacturer William Allan Coats (1853–1926) had purchased it in 1907 for £165. Burrell hung it in his billiard room at Hutton Castle where it was singled out for praise in July 1934 by the French antiquarian and art dealer Jacques Seligmann (1858–1923).

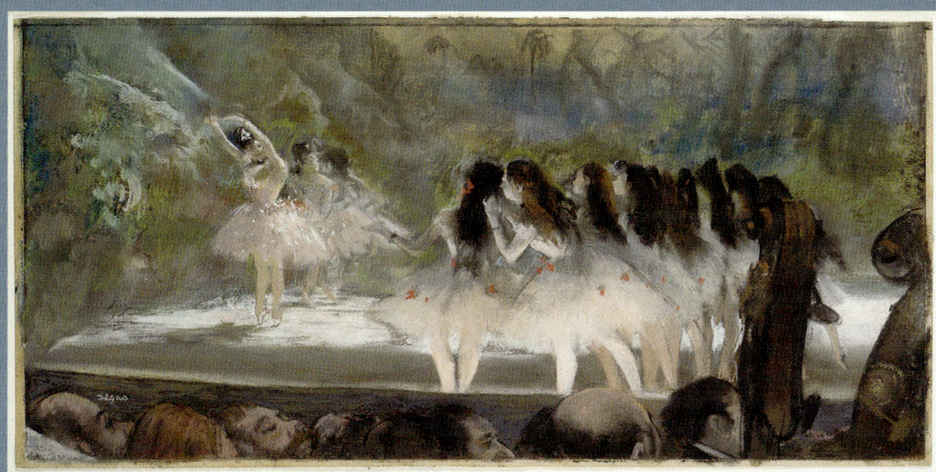

_Ballet at the Paris Opéra_, 1877, by Edgar Degas, pastel over monotype on paper. The Art Institute of Chicago, 1981.12.

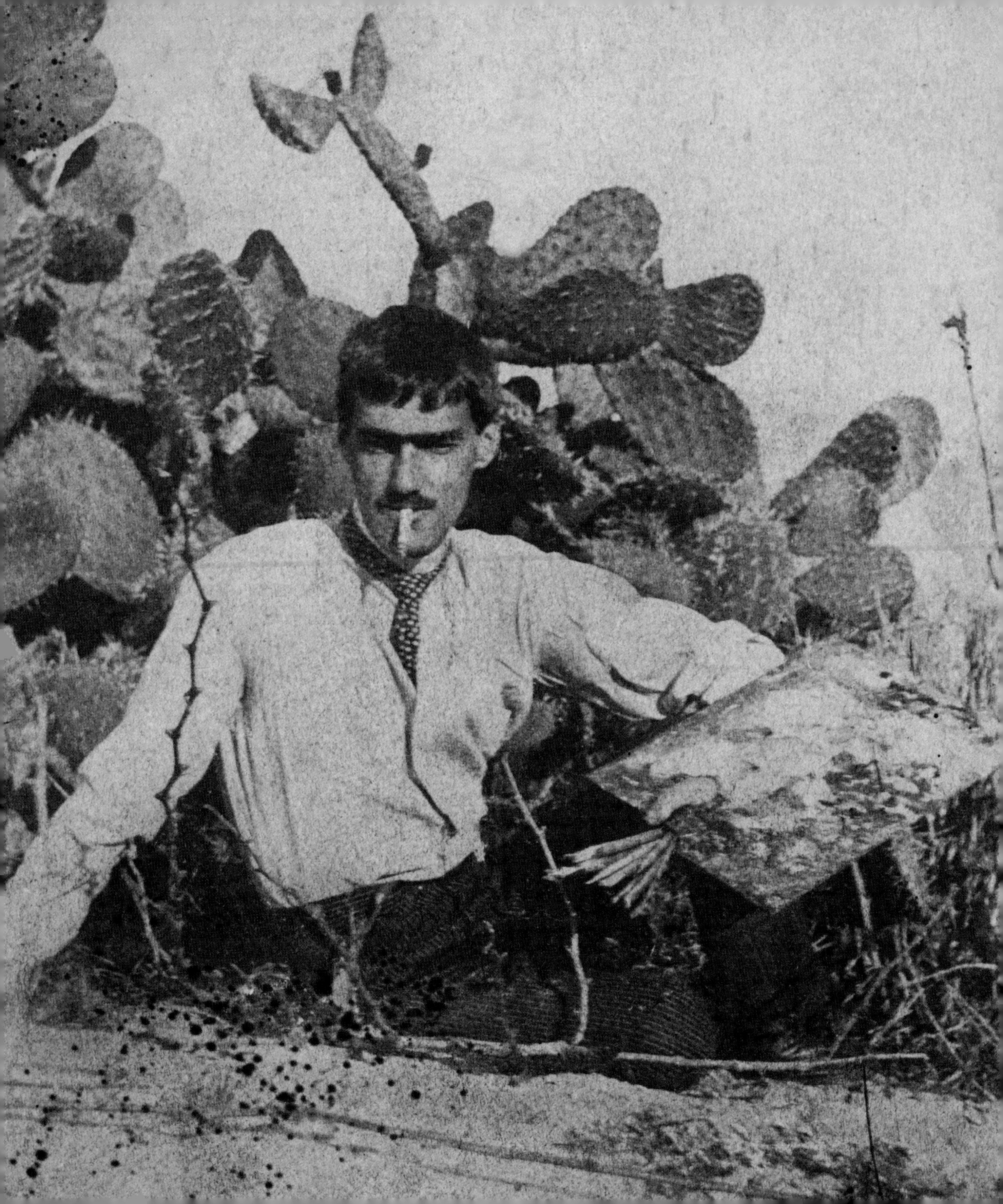

# Travels in Morocco and Spain

Throughout the nineteenth century Spain and Morocco held a fascination for British artists and writers, drawn by their unique cultures and traditions, rich art and architecture, distinctive landscapes, intense light and warm climates, and by the excitement of travelling off the main tourist route. Crawhall was encouraged to journey to Morocco because of the relatively low cost of living and availability of horses. He was also motivated by health reasons, suffering from long-term lung problems. He may have visited Tangier as early as 1882. He was certainly there by 1884, when he also visited Spain. Until the mid 1890s he returned to winter annually at the Moroccan port, sometimes for six months at a time.

With its walled medina, whitewashed buildings, narrow cobbled streets and bustling markets, Tangier inspired many artists. At the time Europe was colonizing Africa, but Morocco remained independent with extensive diplomatic and military support from Britain. Tangier was full of European diplomats. The adventurer, politician and writer RB Cunninghame Graham (1852–1936) described it as 'one of the most fascinating places in the whole world to live in'. However, Crawhall was more interested in depicting its animal life – camels, mules, oxen, goats, wild dogs, and particularly horses.

Crawhall fitted in well with the elite European community in Tangier, with its busy sporting and social calendar. He enthusiastically took part in its polo matches, horseraces, gymkhanas and athletic meets. He joined the Tangier Hunt with its mongrel 'hounds', where he was first whip to the charismatic

Spanish nobleman Don Bernardino Fernández de Velasco, sixteenth Duke of Frías (1866–1916). His circle also included Lavery and Scottish sporting artist George Denholm Armour (1864–1949), and from time to time Melville and William Kennedy. Crawhall took part in amateur bullfights and 'pig-sticking' (wild boar hunting). The latter was typical of the cultural insensitivity of Europeans at the time in this predominantly Muslim country; Frías writes of making local villagers act as beaters. Many of Crawhall's sketches reflect the prevailing Imperialist and racist attitudes of Europeans in Africa.

From Tangier, Crawhall found he could easily travel to Spain, taking a paddle steamer to Gibraltar and then on to Andalusia. There it was not the Hispano-Moresque architecture, dramatic sierras, colourful fiestas or seductive flamenco that attracted his attention, but the gory spectacle of the bullfight. Walton's portrait of Crawhall (p. 10), inscribed 'MADRID 84', shows him standing beside a painting of a bullfight and bullfighting posters, suggesting that from an early date Spain and the tense excitement of the bullfight had a defining impact on him.

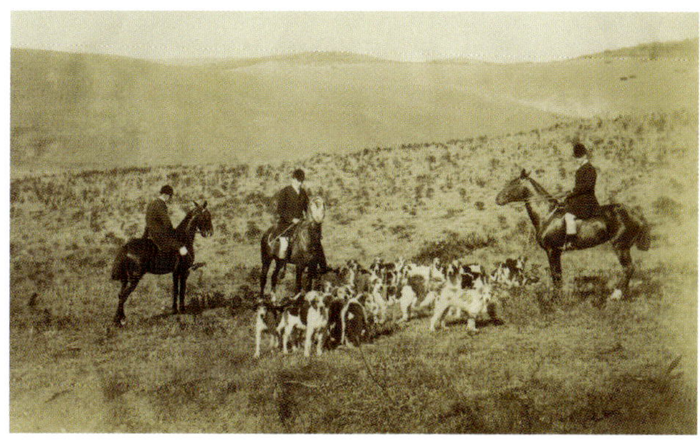

Crawhall, on his favourite horse Dan Dancer, hunting near Tangier around 1892–93 with his artist friends Armour and Robert Bevan (1865–1925). Tate Archive, London, M04952.

Opposite: Crawhall poses with oil palette and brushes for a staged photograph in Morocco, about 1884. In fact, he used watercolour, not oil, and preferred to paint in the studio rather than out of doors. Private collection.

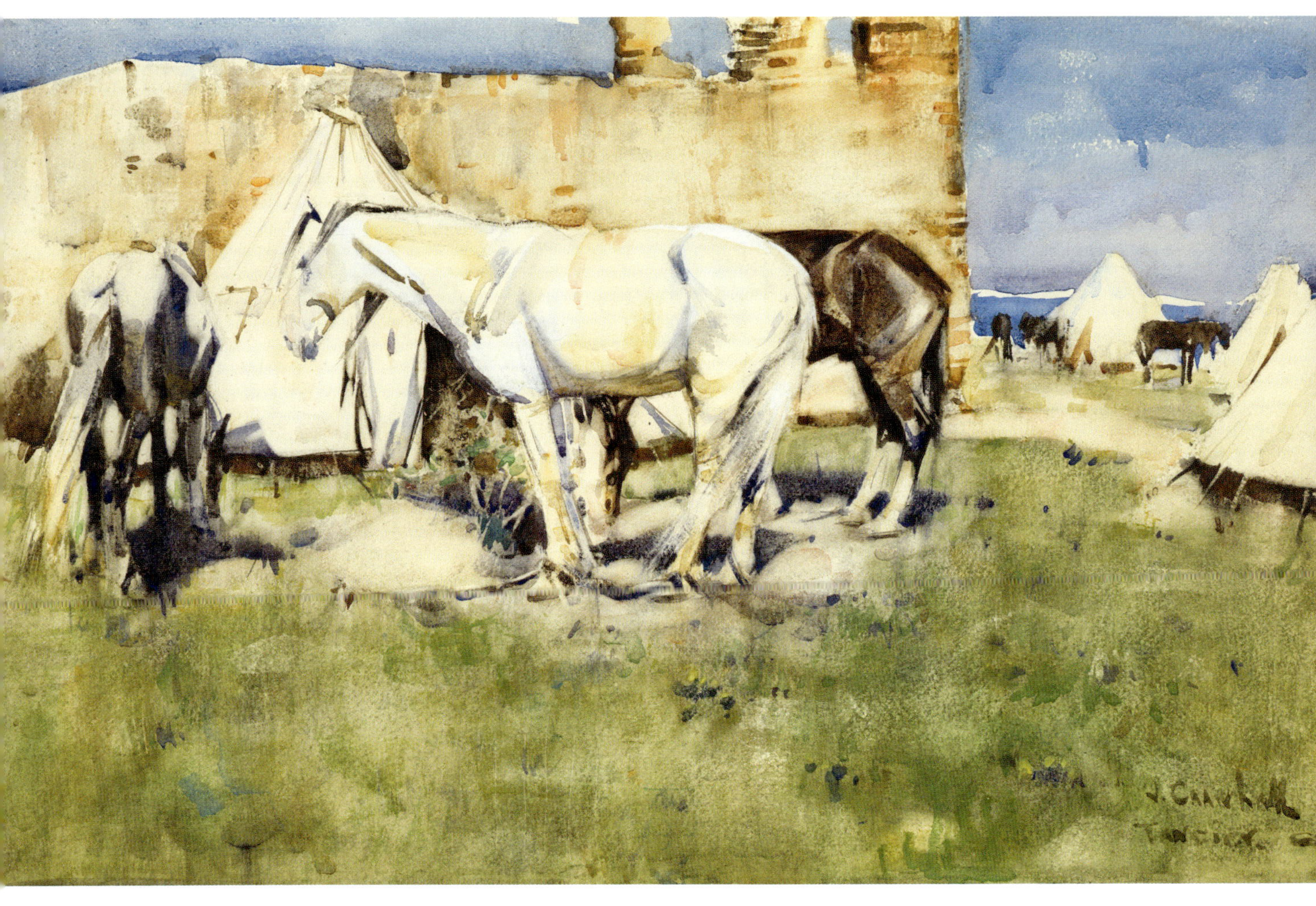

**_Picketed Horses, Tangier,_** 1888
Watercolour on paper
31.2 x 49.6 cm
35.137

According to Cunninghame Graham, 'No place could have suited him [Crawhall] better than the Tangier of those days. In it he found exactly what he wanted for his art.' This primarily involved horses, which in Morocco could be bought cheaply and kept for under a shilling per day. Crawhall acquired an old gelding, Dan Dancer, a cross between a north African Barb and a Spanish mare, who had apparently once pulled a cab in Gibraltar and had great stamina. Crawhall was a skilled horseman. Whether riding a borrowed prize stallion or his own Dan Dancer, he inevitably came first in any race.

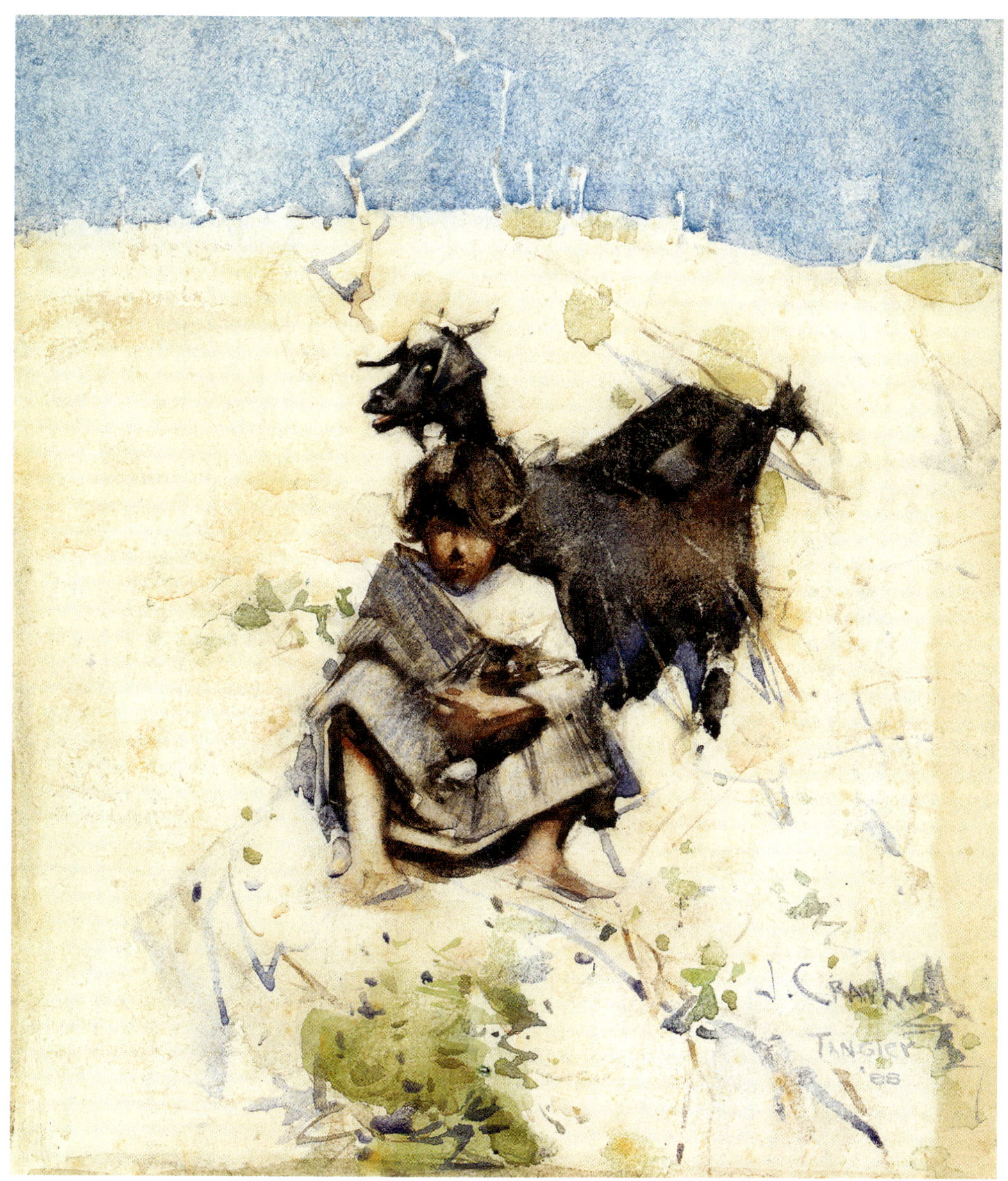

***The Goatherd,*** 1888
Watercolour on paper
25.8 x 22.5 cm
35.128

It was in Morocco that Crawhall perfected his watercolour technique. The arid landscape and brilliant light took some adjusting to but Crawhall revelled in the extremity of the contrasts. The environment encouraged him to be more radical in his abbreviation. Here boy and goat are summarily delineated, and the background is left uncompromisingly empty. The textured paper itself is used to evoke the dry, barren ground. However, the redaction was too extreme for some. *The Glasgow Herald* wrote of *The Goatherd* on 28 November 1888: 'Art cannot be reduced to mere vague suggestion, and Mr Crawhall's sketches are nothing more.'

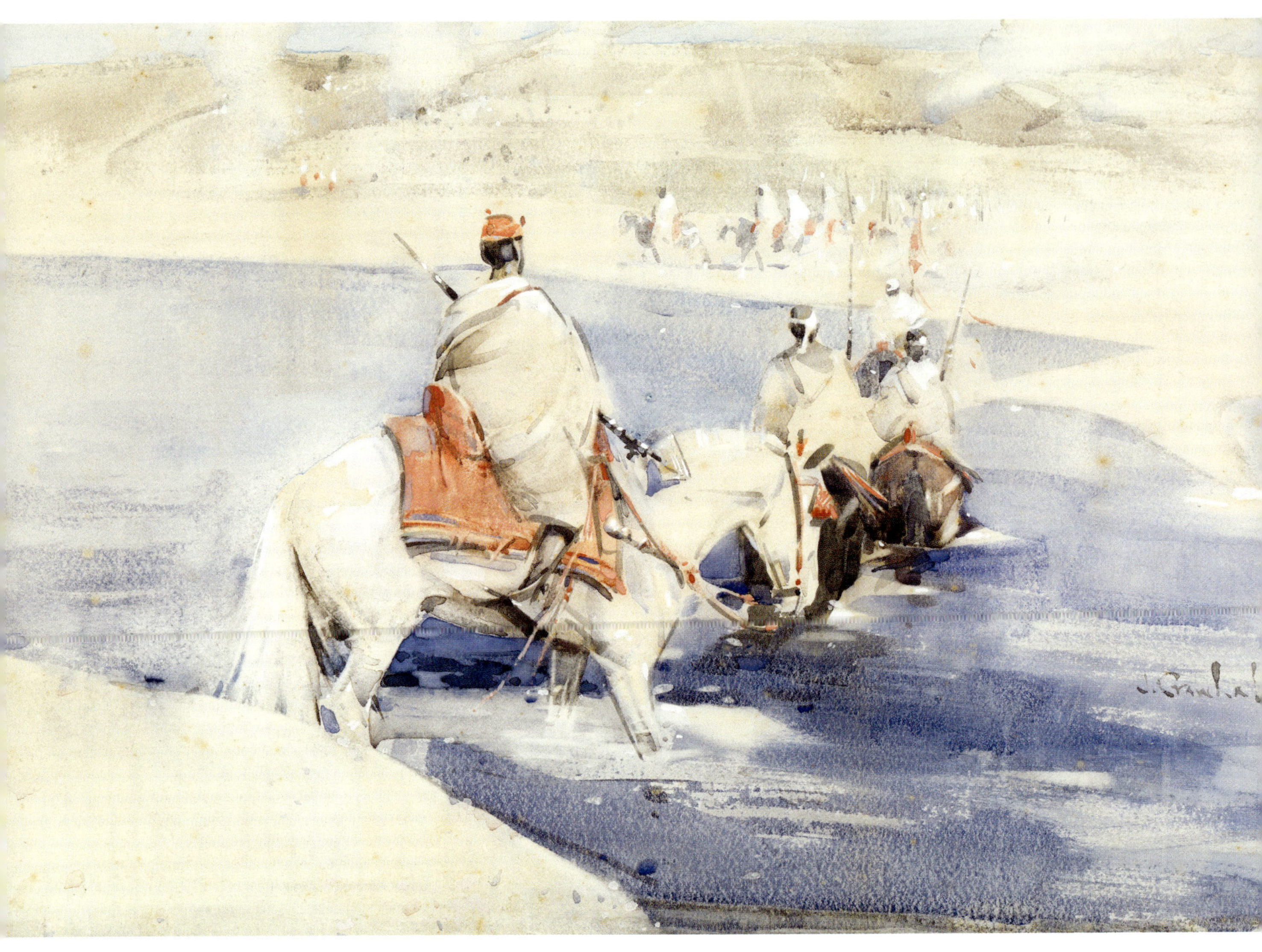

### *An Arab Raid,* about 1888
Watercolour and bodycolour on paper
29.6 x 41.5 cm
35.76

As part of the European community in Tangier, Crawhall lived a privileged life removed from the realities of Moroccan poverty and political unrest. However, this painting may show a violent encounter he and Armour witnessed, between mounted soldiers of the sultan of Morocco, Hassan I (1836–94), and a group of Riffians, Berber-speaking people, over unpaid taxes. The smoke rising in the distance indicates the position of the Riffians, as described by Armour: 'we hardly saw any of the defenders, though the smoke of their black powder showed where they were ... many villages were burned'.

With its bold diagonal format, the deep azure blue of the river daringly contrasted with areas of empty space and bare paper, this work prefigures Melville's watercolours of Spain and North Africa from the 1890s.

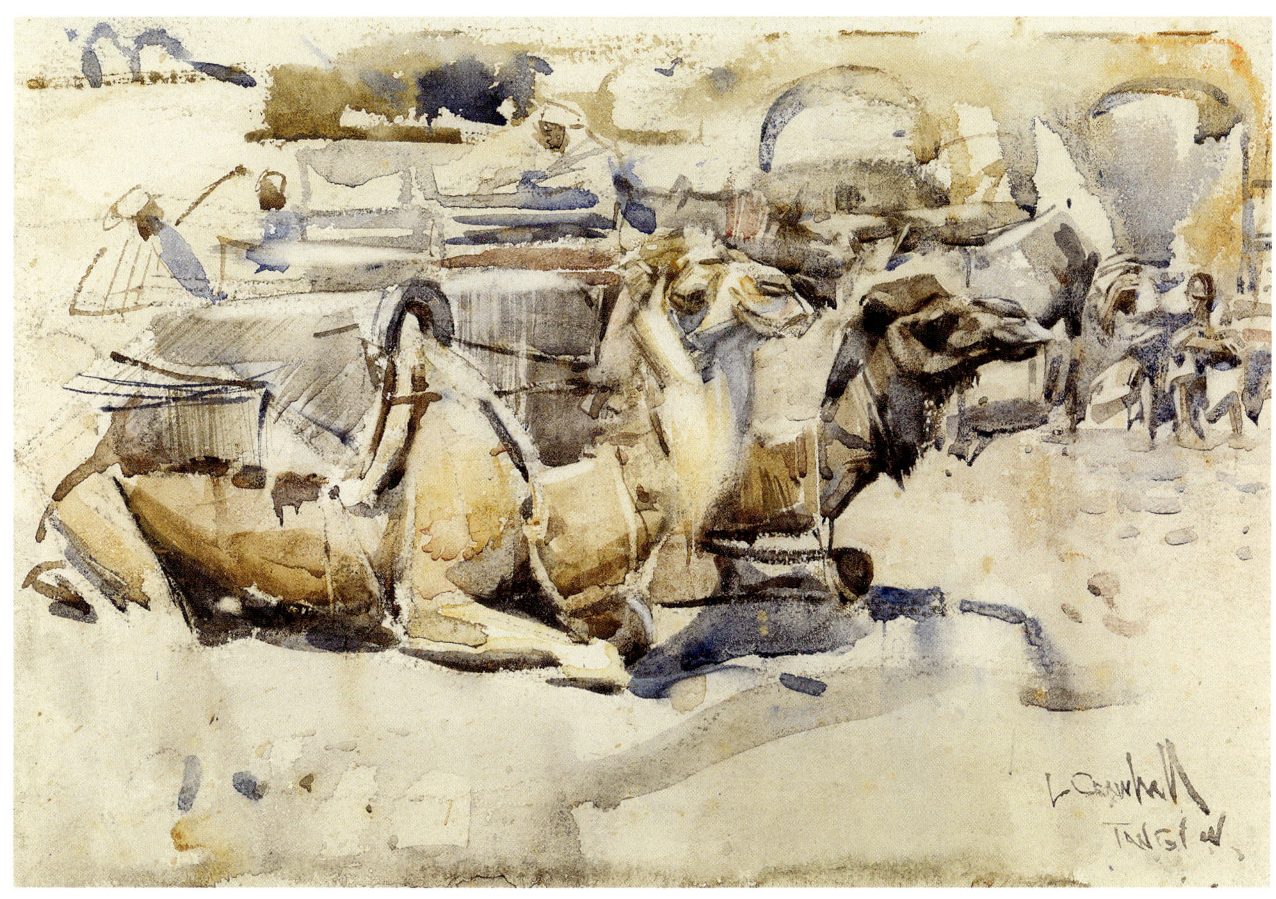

***Camels, the Socco, Tangier,*** 1888
Watercolour on paper
22.3 x 33.1 cm
35.94

The Grand Socco in the centre of Tangier was a large busy marketplace. It would have been full of animals, stalls and people shouting as they bought and sold their wares. However, in this watercolour, Crawhall marginalized human activity, the few figures depicted abbreviated to an unprecedented degree. He focused on a group of camels sitting sedately in front of the market's distinctive double-gate. Although the animals' heads are described with great accuracy, Crawhall allowed the blues and browns to run and blur in an apparently chaotic way.

When this painting was exhibited in Newcastle in 1888, a reviewer noted, 'Mr Crawhall has succeeded in giving a twofold impression of obscurity arising from excessive light on the one hand and marvellous arrangements of colour on the other'. Thomas Campbell Mackie (1886–1952), Head of Design at Glasgow School of Art, described it as 'one of the most wonderful pieces of broad impressionism that was ever executed'.

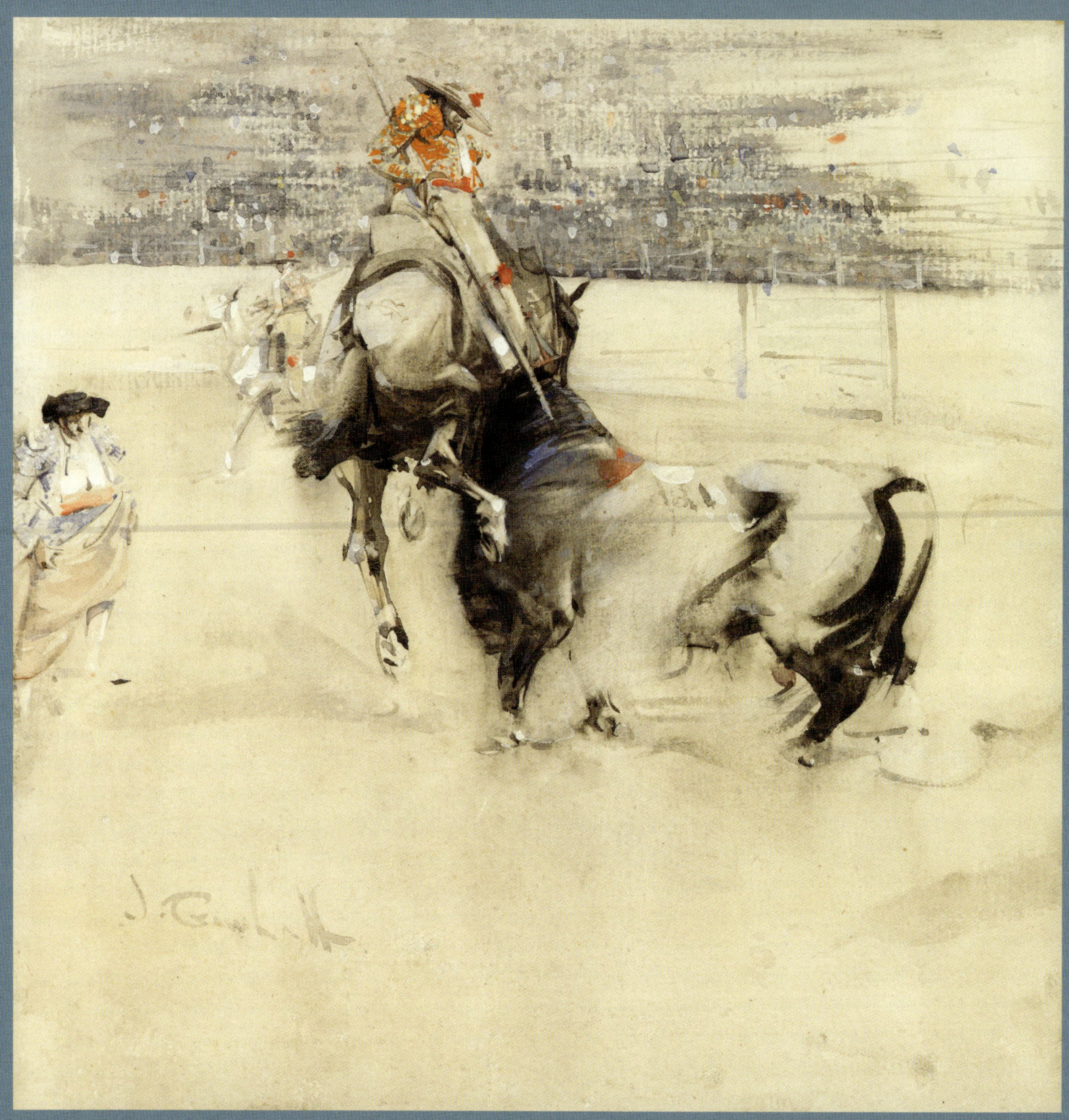

# Artwork in Focus

***Bullfight at Algeciras,*** about 1889–91
Watercolour and bodycolour on paper
37.5 x 34.9 cm
35.85

From Tangier Crawhall travelled with friends to Algeciras in Andalusia to visit the annual June fair, the *Feria Real de Algeciras*, at which there was a cattle market, stalls and fairground. However, they went primarily to see its bullfight, known for having the best matadors and bulls in Spain.

Despite expressing revulsion at the suffering of horses within bullfights, Crawhall here chose to depict the moment when the picador's mount is lifted off the ground by the bull. It is unclear if the horse's unprotected belly is being gored, but its anguish is apparent as it lunges and kicks out. The crowd is a blur in the background; Crawhall focuses our attention on the movement and energy of the fight, the picador twisting in the saddle to lance the bull in the neck. The dust kicked up around the bull suggests the speed and power of the its charge. *The Scottish Art Review* described the work as 'almost too painfully realistic'. A masterpiece of atmosphere and emotion, Crawhall conveys the tension and passion of the bullfight, as though the viewer were experiencing the life and death struggle between horse, picador and bull first-hand.

*'Five of us made a rather memorable expedition to the annual fair at Algeciras, our chief purpose being to see a bull-fight … The whole proceedings of the bull-ring have been so often described that I shall only say that it struck me as one of the most stirring spectacles I have ever seen, despite the horror that the horse part makes one feel … Crawhall afterwards painted a very fine picture of a picador and a bull …'*

George Armour, *Bridle and Brush: Reminiscences of an Artist Sportsman*, 1937

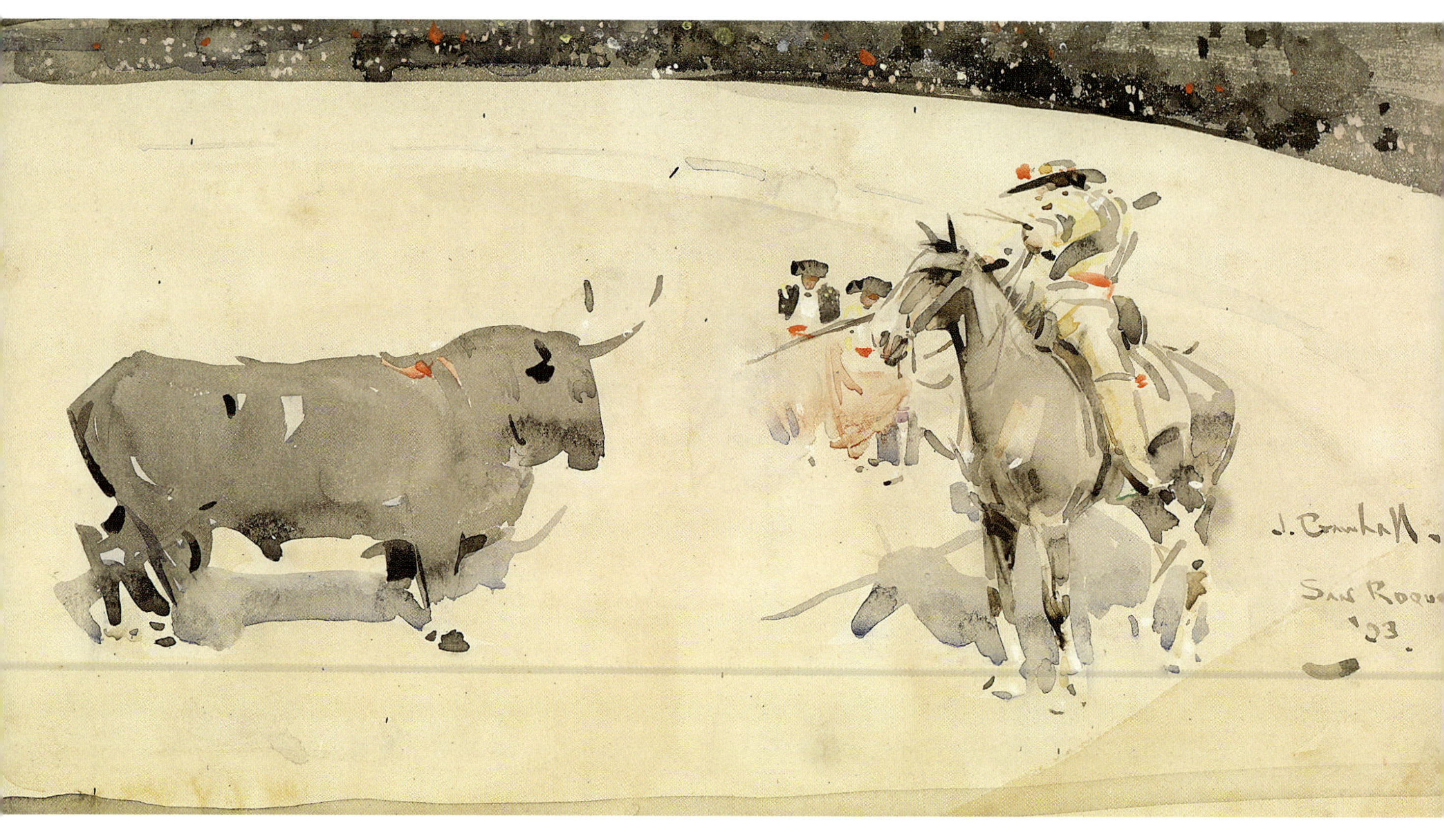

**Bullfight – San Roque,** 1893
Watercolour and bodycolour on paper
22.3 x 40.7 cm
35.86

San Roque, in the province of Cádiz, is a small hilltop town to the north of Algeciras and the Gibraltar peninsula. Crawhall visited its bullring, one of the oldest in Andalusia, in 1893. In this work he again focuses on a tense encounter between bull and picador. The red on the bull's shoulder indicates it has already sustained injury. Enraged, it paws the ground, suggested by the multiple positioning of the right hind leg and scumbled bodycolour. Leaning back, the picador points his lance threateningly. Two assistants stand ready to deflect the bull. Crawhall uses the curve of the arena to enclose the action and concentrate attention on the power of the bull, beside which the bullfighters look slight and insubstantial.

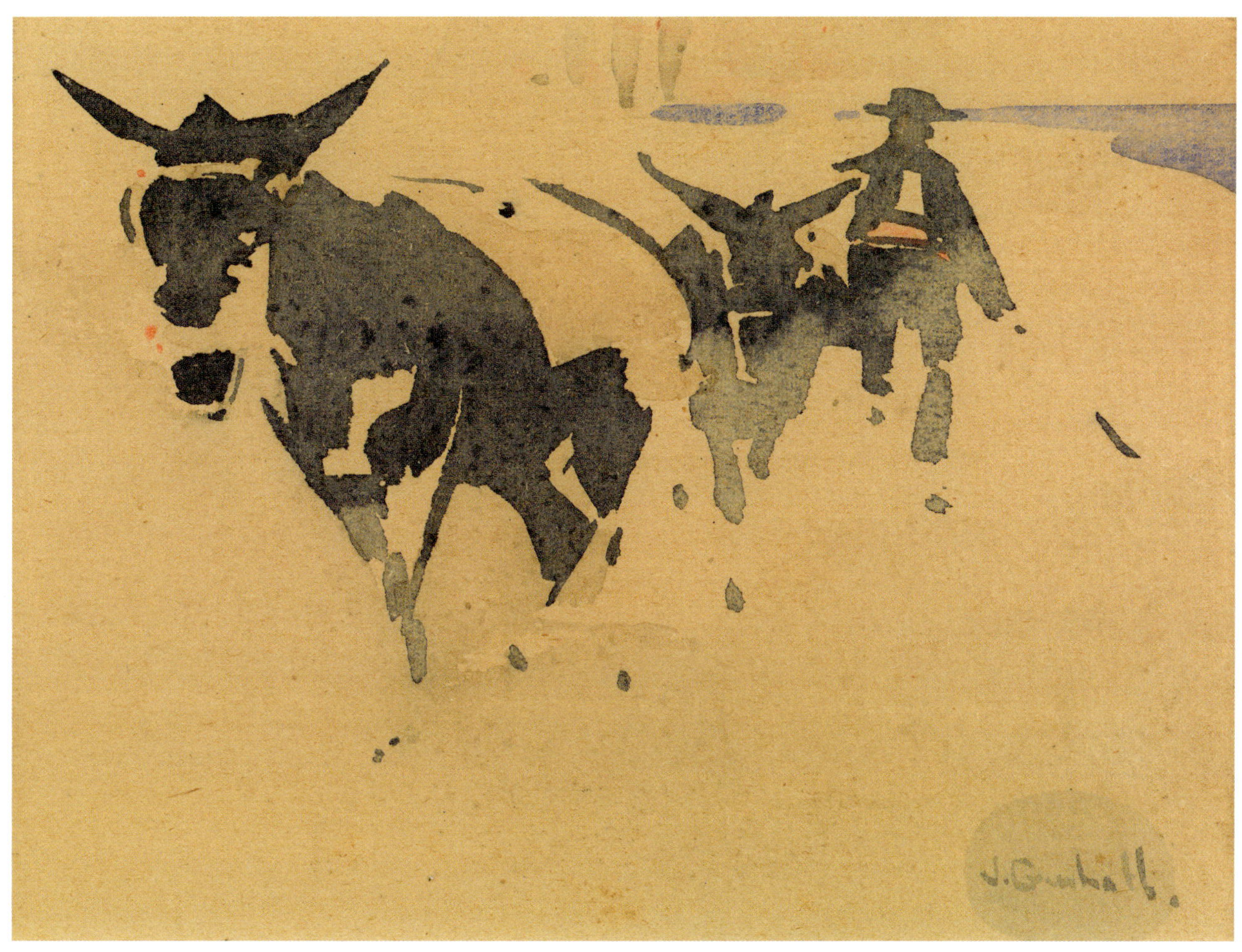

## *Mules on the Sand at Tangier,* about 1896

Watercolour on paper
13.5 x 20.2 cm
35.162

This watercolour is astounding in its visual economy and brilliance of elision. Crawhall allows the tinted paper to do most of the work, the two mules and their driver suggested with the barest of form. Their black silhouettes are touched with pink and blue to indicate bridles and the driver's sash. The sea is a strip of blue in the distance. Despite the lack of modelling, there is still a convincing sense of recession into space. The whole is very effective, the dramatic simplicity of the contrasts conveying the glare of desert sun, when detail is lost and all appears mirage-like.

This portrait shows Crawhall in racing colours. Artist Thomas Campbell Mackie observed admiringly in 1922: 'He was both physically and artistically a light-weight, but never jockey of that sort rode more surely to victory'. *Joseph Crawhall*, about 1896–98, by George Denholm Armour, oil on canvas, reproduced in his memoir *Bridle and Brush: Reminiscences of an Artist Sportsman*, 1937.

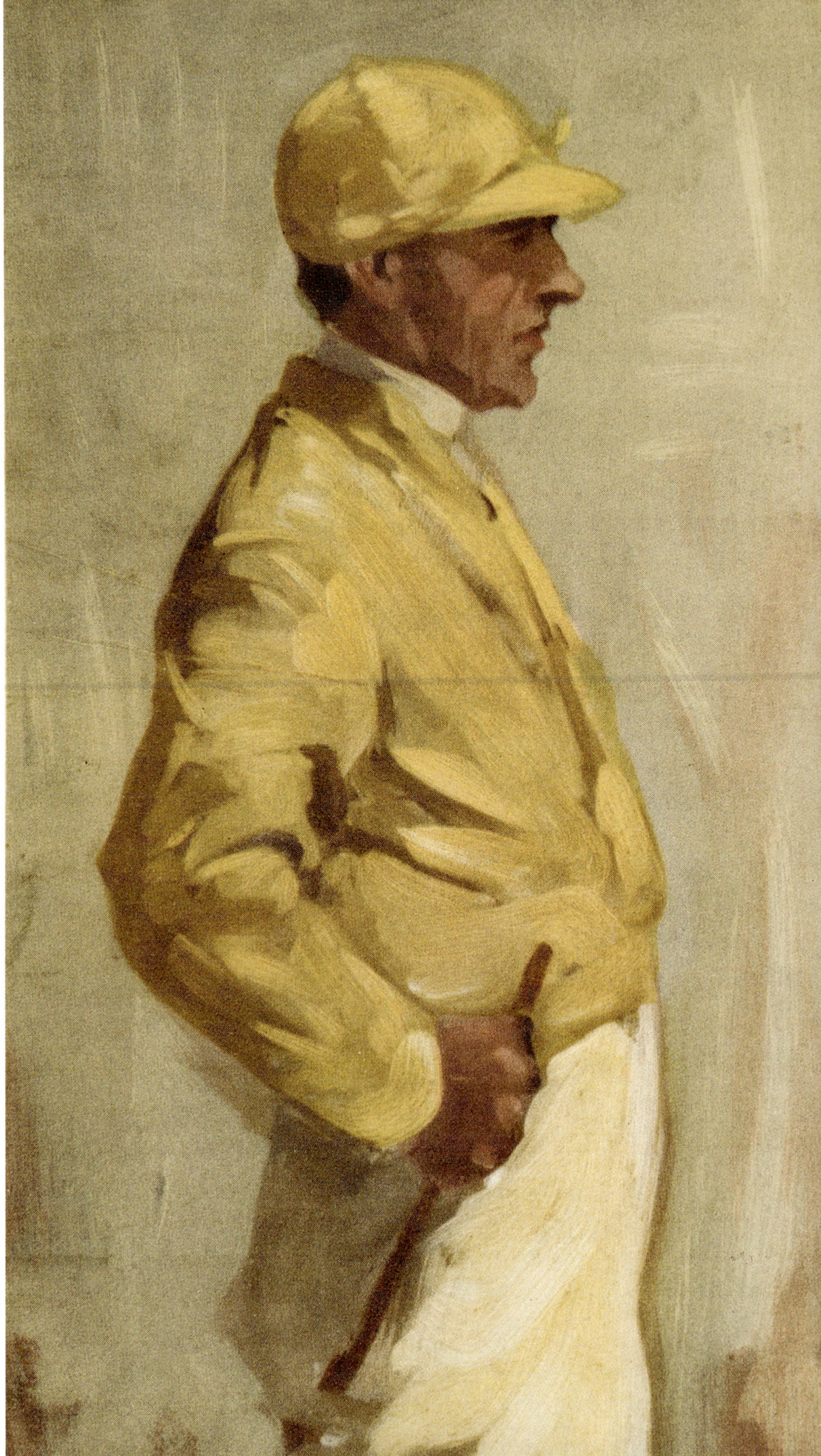

# Horses

Crawhall's best artwork features horses – thoroughbreds with pent-up pre-race nerves, calm cross-country hunters, stumpy work ponies, prim carriage horses, disciplined performance animals, fiery Barb stallions, tensed toreador geldings, protective mares with their foals. He studied and observed their individual traits and idiosyncrasies, describing their distinctive gaits and stances, telling a story through a mere hang of a lip, flick of the tail or flex of a hind leg. His agility in drawing came from familiarity. His family were keen sportspeople and he grew up on horseback. His contemporaries commented on his slightly bandy legs, a result of riding from too young an age. He would joke that 'Providence would have bestowed four legs on man had he intended him to go afoot.' Wherever he lived, Newcastle, Tangier, Hertfordshire or Yorkshire, Crawhall rode, took part in local hunts – then both legal and more widely accepted than now – and attended horse fairs and race meets. He also competed. His friend Armour wrote that Crawhall was 'a beautiful natural horseman, and in Tangier was our champion jockey'.

Around 1896–98 Crawhall ran a stud farm with Armour in Wheathampstead, Hertfordshire. Armour recalled: 'Our experience of horse-buying in Morocco still influenced our ideas of price, and we really had some wonderful bargains.' For fun they used to enter flapper meetings, that is, unlicensed pony racing competitions, covering their expenses through small wins. Crawhall rode a small but spirited Barb stallion called Mesmuda, which he had imported from Tangier. From 1903 he lived with his family in Brandsby, near Easingwold, in North Yorkshire, where he continued to breed hunters and racehorses.

Many of Crawhall's relationships were based around a shared love of horses, whether Alexander Reid, with whom he used to ride in Glasgow, or friends like Lavery or Cunninghame Graham, with whom he rode and hunted in Tangier. Many of his wealthy patrons, including the Burrells, hunted and attended the races. The Eglinton Hunt met at Perceton House, the Ayrshire home of Burrell's sister Mary Mitchell (1873–1964). Gordon Burrell (1895–1949), Burrell's nephew, and his wife Brenda (née Bibby; 1887–1959) owned thoroughbreds which would compete at Ayr and Musselburgh racecourses. At Hutton Castle in Berwickshire, Burrell himself rode and hunted, renting Mayshiel Estate in the Lammermuirs for grouse shooting. Crawhall's equine watercolours and drawings portrayed a world that the Burrells understood and to which they related.

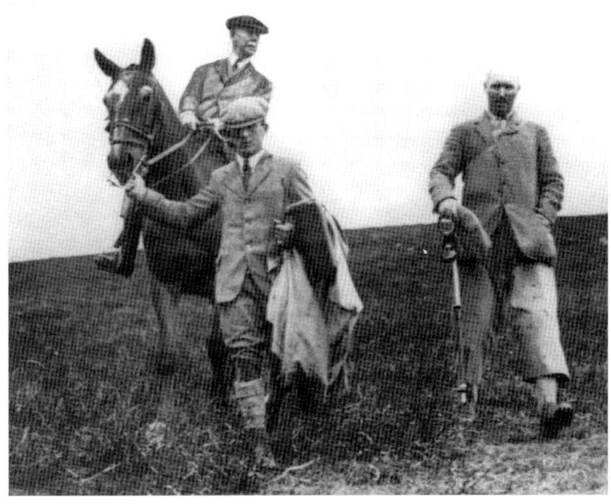

William Burrell on horseback with his gillie, accompanied by horse and cattle breeder Edward Kenelm Digby, the 11th Baron Digby (1894–1964), at a shooting party at Mayshiel in 1936. Glasgow Museums Archive, GMA.2013.1.1.464.

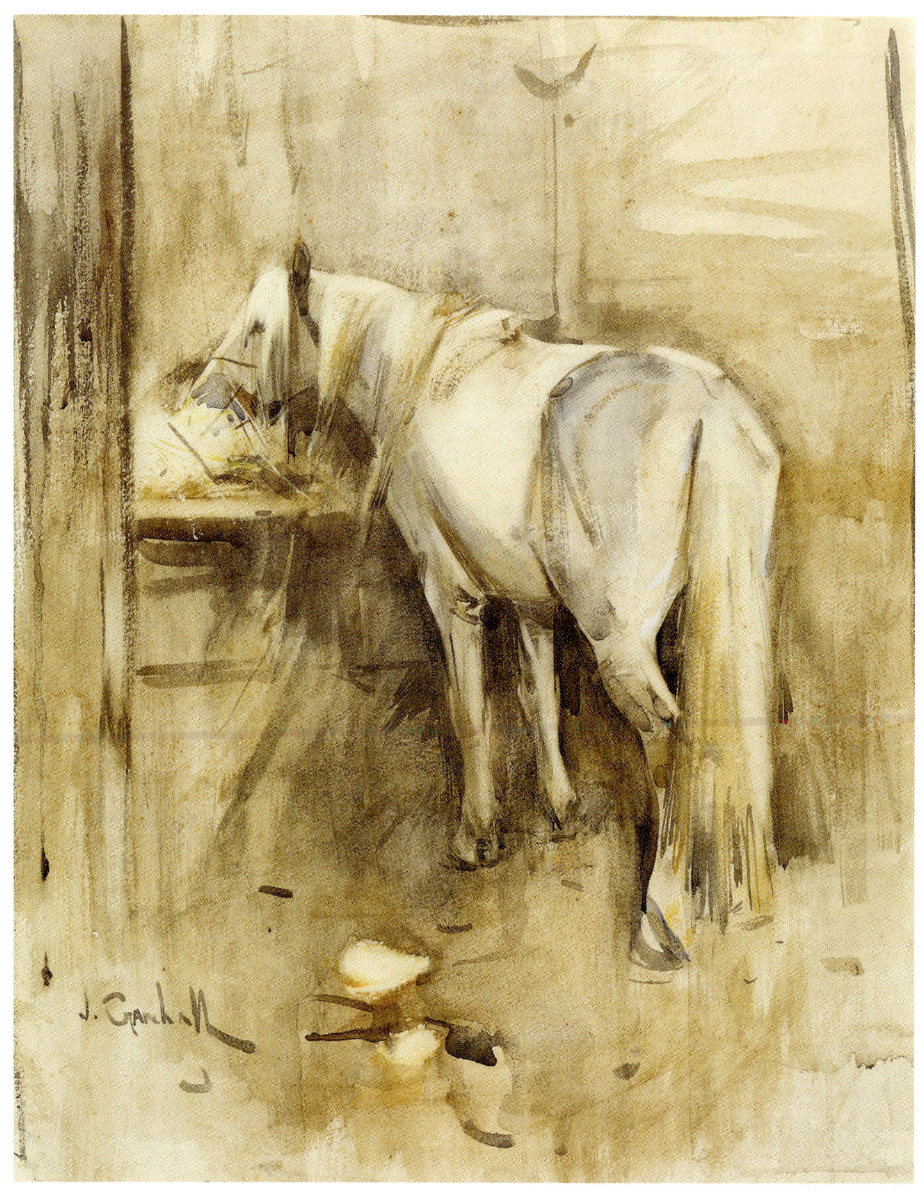

**The White Horse,** 1886
Watercolour and bodycolour on paper
46.2 x 36.3 cm
35.204

This study of a Barb stallion at a stable manger may have been Burrell's first Crawhall purchase. A mere turn of the head and prick of the ears, suggesting the horse registers our presence, typifies the economy and precision of Crawhall's style. From May 1911 Burrell recorded his acquisitions in purchase books with dates, descriptions and prices listed. He bought most of his Crawhalls after this time, but it is hard to know exactly when many earlier acquisitions were made. However, we know that Burrell bought this work for 12 guineas from an exhibition at the Scottish Society of Painters in Watercolour in Glasgow in 1886.

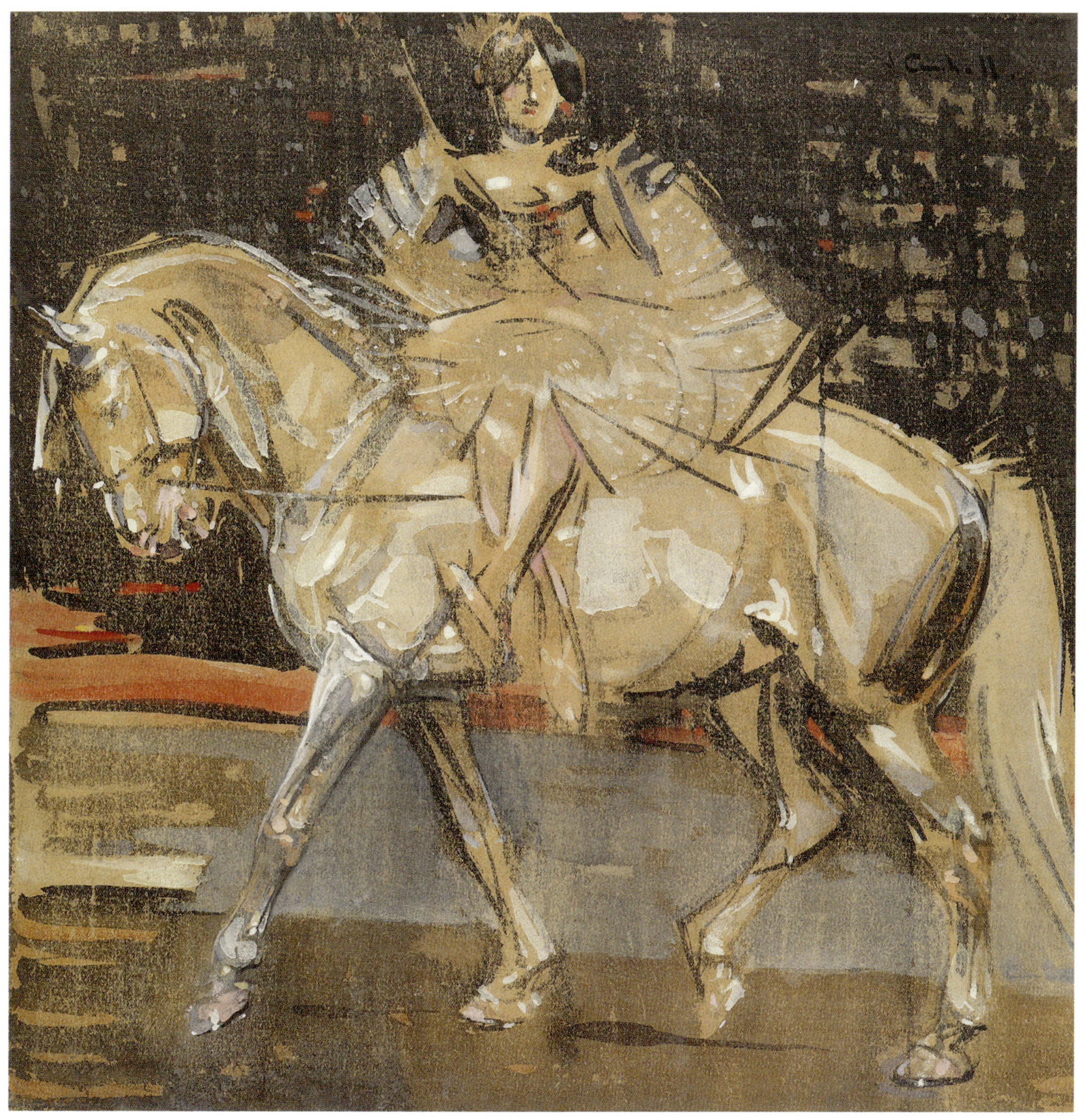

***The Circus Rider,*** about 1908
Bodycolour on paper
41.3 x 39.7 cm
35.100

From childhood Crawhall loved the circus and used to play truant whenever it was in town. The equestrian acrobatics and exotic creatures must have been thrilling to a young boy besotted with animals. This scene may have been inspired by a local circus in Newcastle or perhaps Hengler's Cirque in Glasgow. The golden light falling on horse and rider conveys wonder and awe. Crawhall chose to depict the moment between stunts when, with the rider seated, the horse is the focus of attention. With neck gracefully arched and hooves pointed, the animal moves around the circus ring at a collected trot, to, we can imagine, enthusiastic applause.

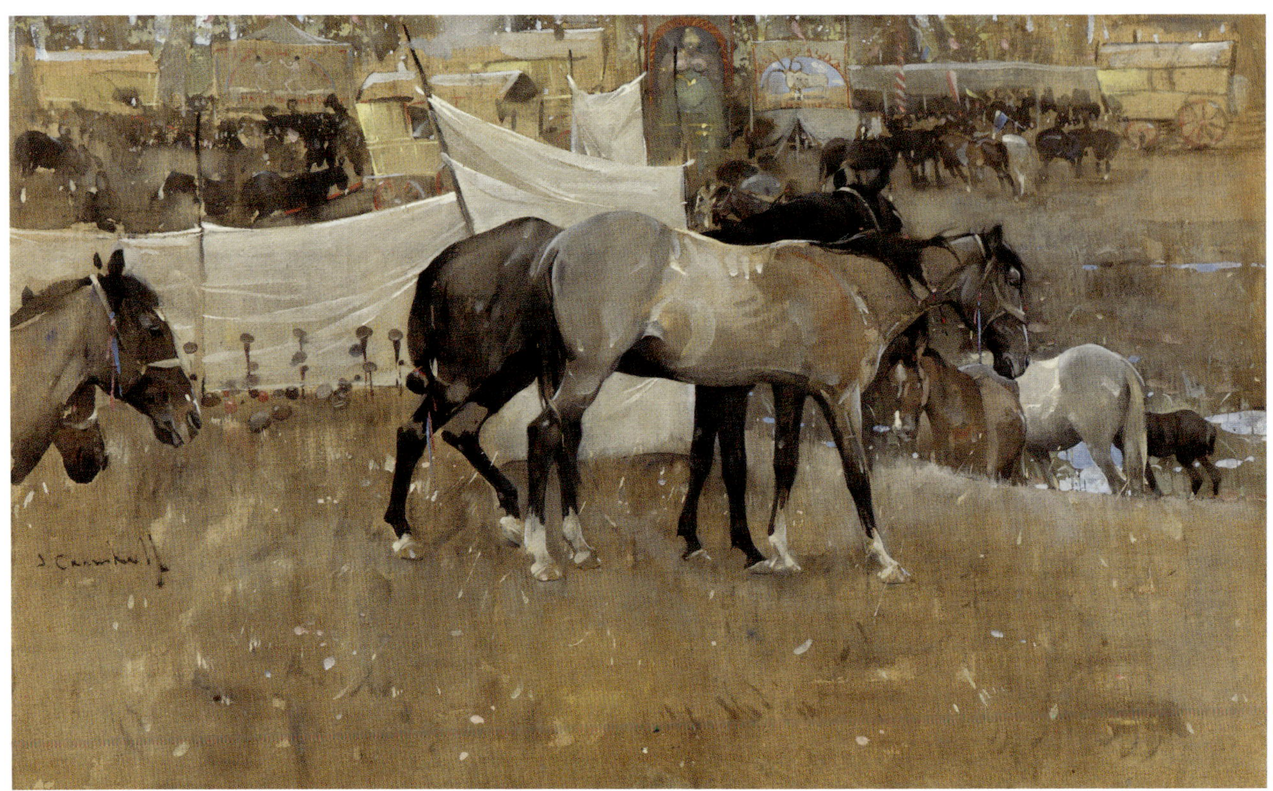

**_Barnet Fair,_** 1893
Bodycolour on linen
36.9 x 59.5 cm
35.80

In the mid 1890s Crawhall and his family lived for a short time in Bayswater, West London, from where they visited the annual September Barnet Fair. There was a livestock sale and funfair with stalls and amusements. In the background of this painting you can see travellers' caravans and sideshows, including boxers and a fat lady, staple elements of a Victorian fairground. However, these are marginalized. The real attraction for Crawhall was the horse market. In the foreground pairs of horses quietly wend their way past the viewer and down the slope, Crawhall noting individual posture and gait.

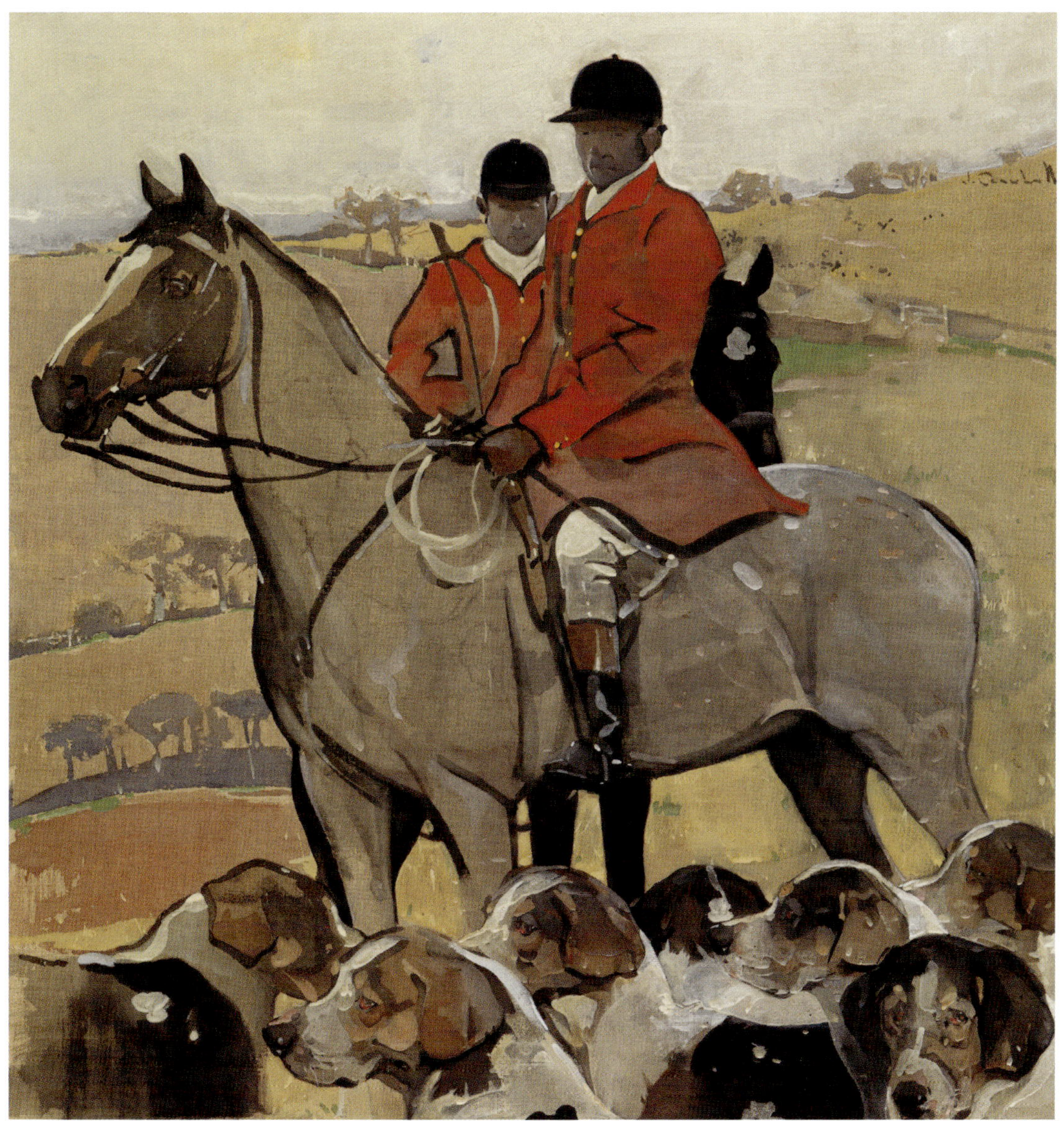

***The Hunt,*** or ***The Meet,*** about 1894–98
Watercolour and bodycolour on linen
66.6 x 64.5 cm
35.156

Crawhall's hunting scenes were not about recording specific events – design considerations were always paramount. Here the red of the huntsmen's coats are perfectly balanced against the gold and lilac tones of the dun horse in near-profile and the stylized agricultural landscape beyond. The alert poise of the horse's ears, the flare of its nostrils and the way it holds the bit of the bridle in its mouth are not carefully observed in a way particular to this scene, but rather show Crawhall's innate understanding and experience of horses over many years, distilled into this image. The result is fluid and bold like poster design with which many artists were experimenting in the 1890s.

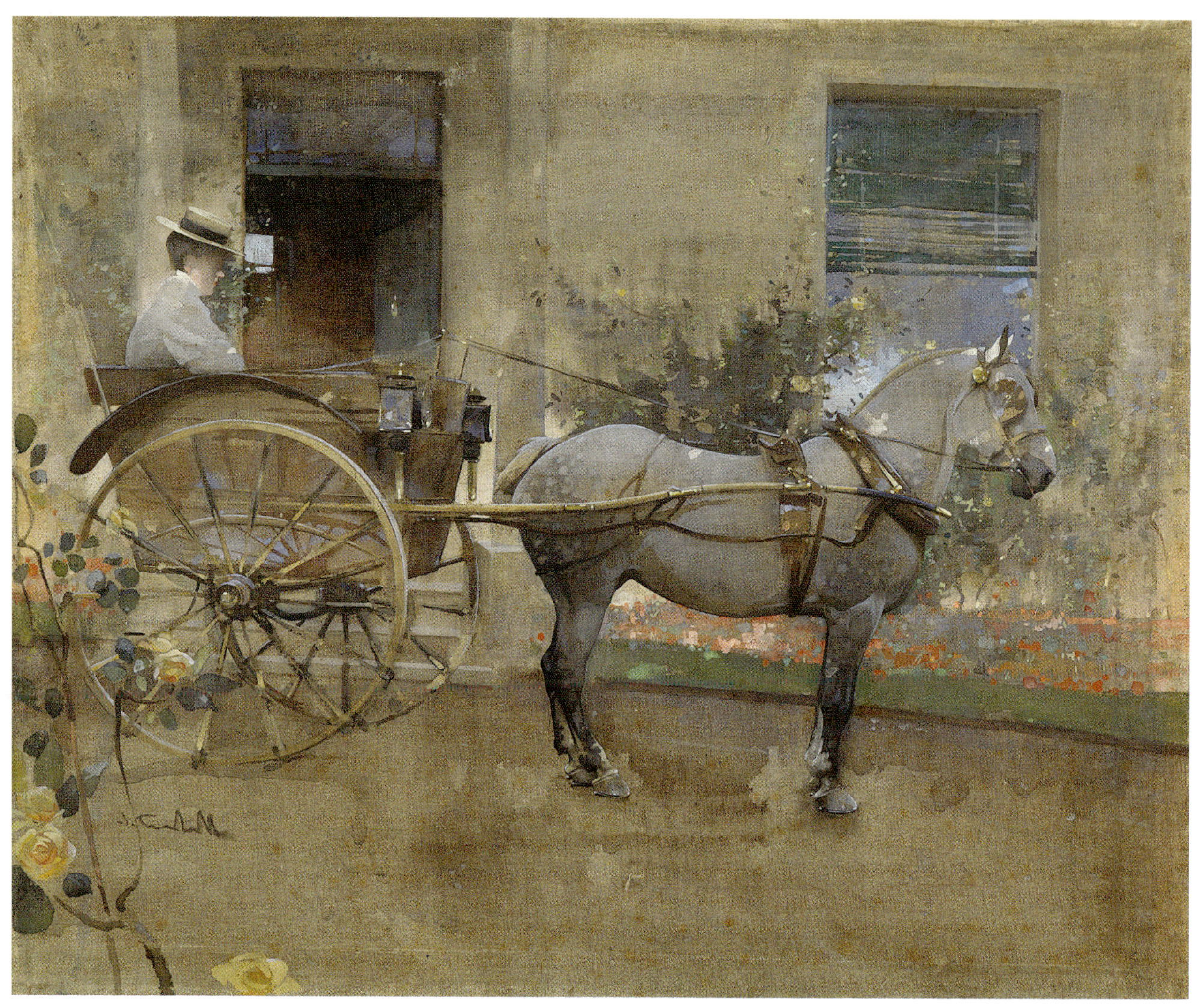

***The Governess Cart,*** about 1899–1900
Watercolour and bodycolour on linen
30.5 x 36.9 cm
35.129

This watercolour probably shows Beacon Banks in Husthwaite, Yorkshire, where Crawhall lived with his mother and sister Beatrice (1866–1930) from 1899. Crawhall often focused on the decorative potential of horse and cart in profile, here set against the curve of the driveway and architectural framework of door, columns and windows. Beatrice is likely to be the driver. The dappled grey mare sets the tone for the elegant muted colour scheme, enhanced by the yellow rosebush in the foreground, typical of the way Japanese artists introduced blossom branches for decorative effect and to suggest pictorial depth.

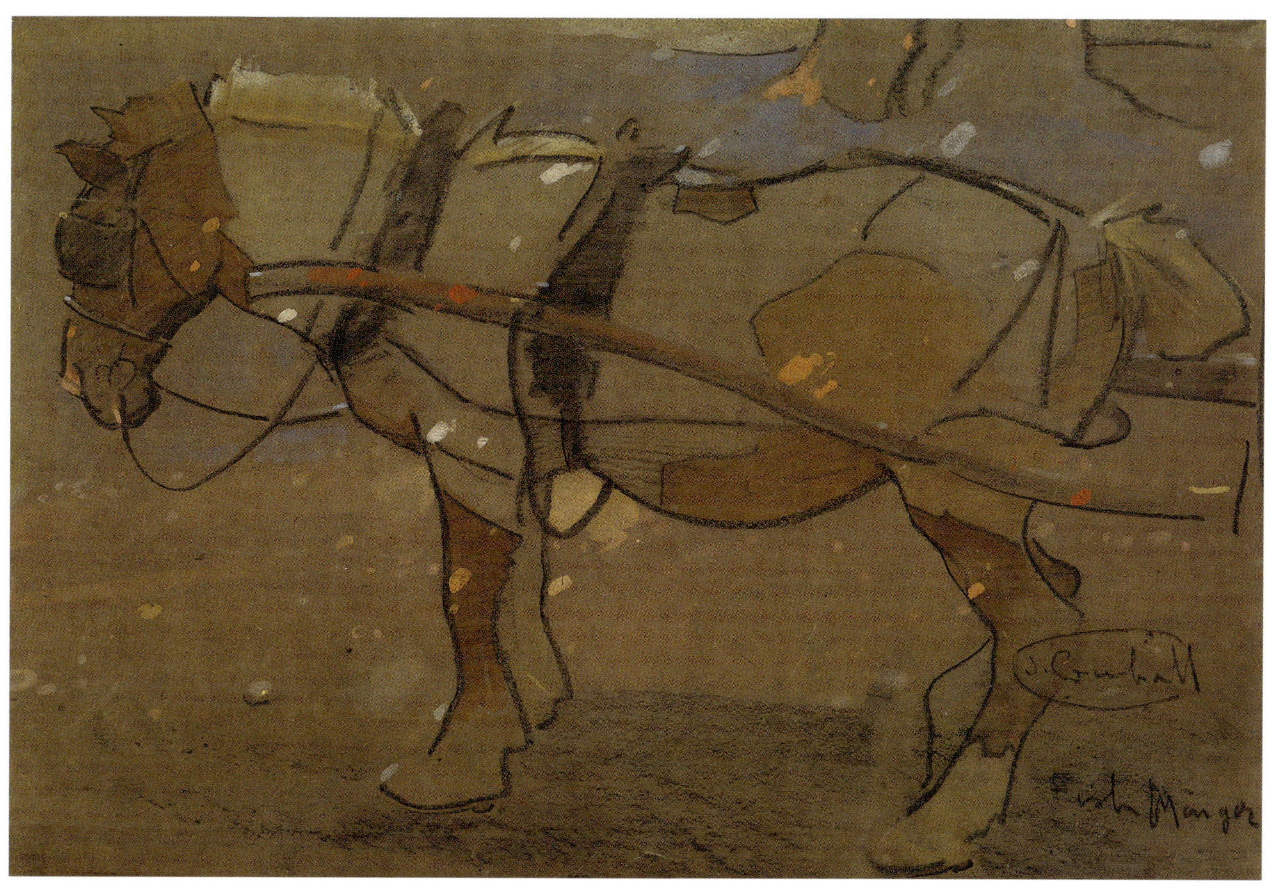

***Fishmonger's Pony,*** about 1896
Chalk, watercolour and bodycolour on paper
24.6 x 35.6 cm
35.116

Crawhall sympathetically depicts the short stocky legs and hollowed back of this working pony, its tired blinkered head bowed under its load, as it waits to take the strain again. The rough brown paper fits the humble subject matter. Despite the poverty of the situation, Crawhall finds beauty in the gentle arabesques of the cart shafts which accentuate the curvature of the horse's rump, belly and neck, the pattern of its skewbald markings, the loop of the reins and oval of the harness yoke. The patterning is continued on to the pictorial surface, which is enlivened with touches of orange, red and blue bodycolour that bring decorative unity to the composition.

***The Race,*** about 1890
Watercolour wash and
bodycolour on paper
22.9 x 14 cm
35.180

The radical foreshortening
in this composition draws
attention to the muscle
and strength of the
racehorse, encapsulated
in its powerful
hindquarters. The unusual
viewpoint gives a sense of
thrill and excitement, as if
the viewer were a rider in
the race. The suggestion
of movement is enhanced
by the curve of the
racetrack and the dynamic
depiction of the whip,
reproduced multiple times
to give a sense of passage
through time and space.
Cunninghame Graham
marvelled at Crawhall's
art which was 'so tuned
to modern vision', and
indeed here Crawhall
prefigures the Italian
Futurists' concern to paint
time, the fourth dimension,
by 20 years.

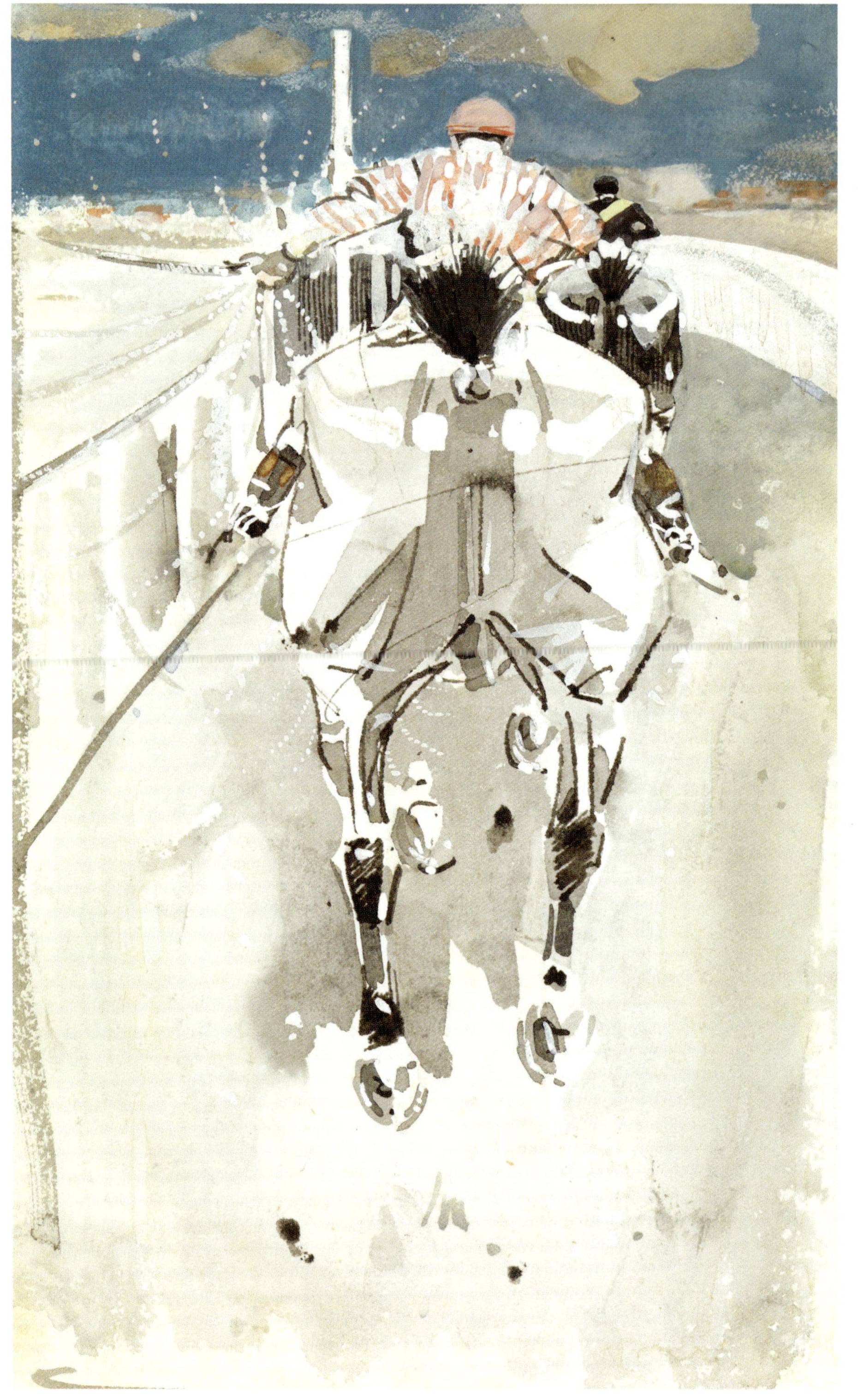

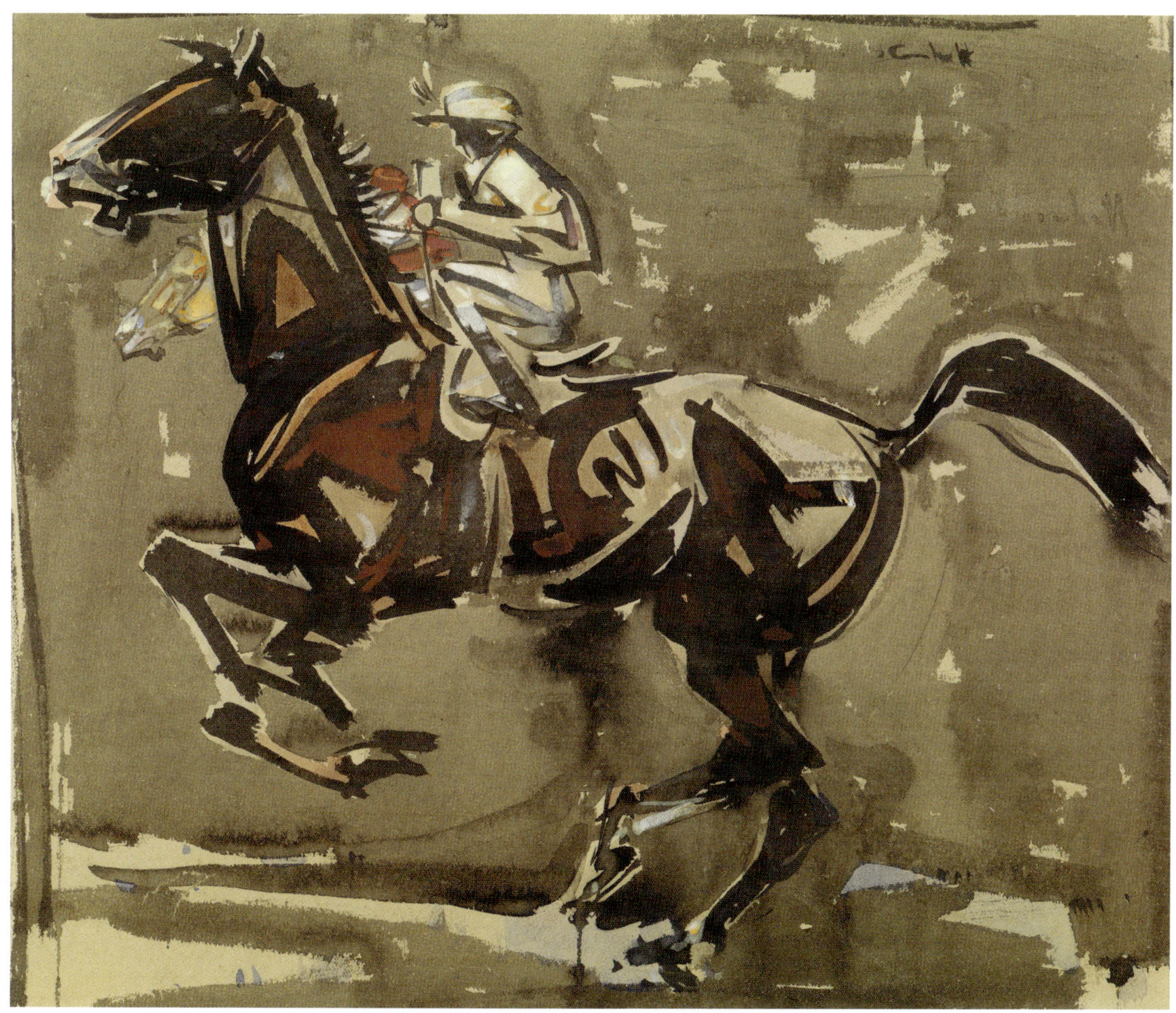

***Tod Sloan – American Jockey,*** about 1899
Bodycolour on paper
33.7 x 38.1 cm
35.195

Racehorse and jockey prepare to jump, movement suggested through a slight blur or afterimage as in photography. From the 1870s there had been experiments with chronophotography, most famously by pioneer British photographer Eadweard Muybridge (1830–1904), who captured galloping horses in successive frames, pre-dating actual moving film. Crawhall, one of the first artists to accurately depict a horse in motion, would have been aware of such experimental photography, which was also used to record horseraces.

In this work he centres on the unique riding style of celebrity American jockey James Forman 'Tod' Sloan (1874–1933), who revolutionized British horseracing from 1897, crouching in the saddle with short reins and stirrups.

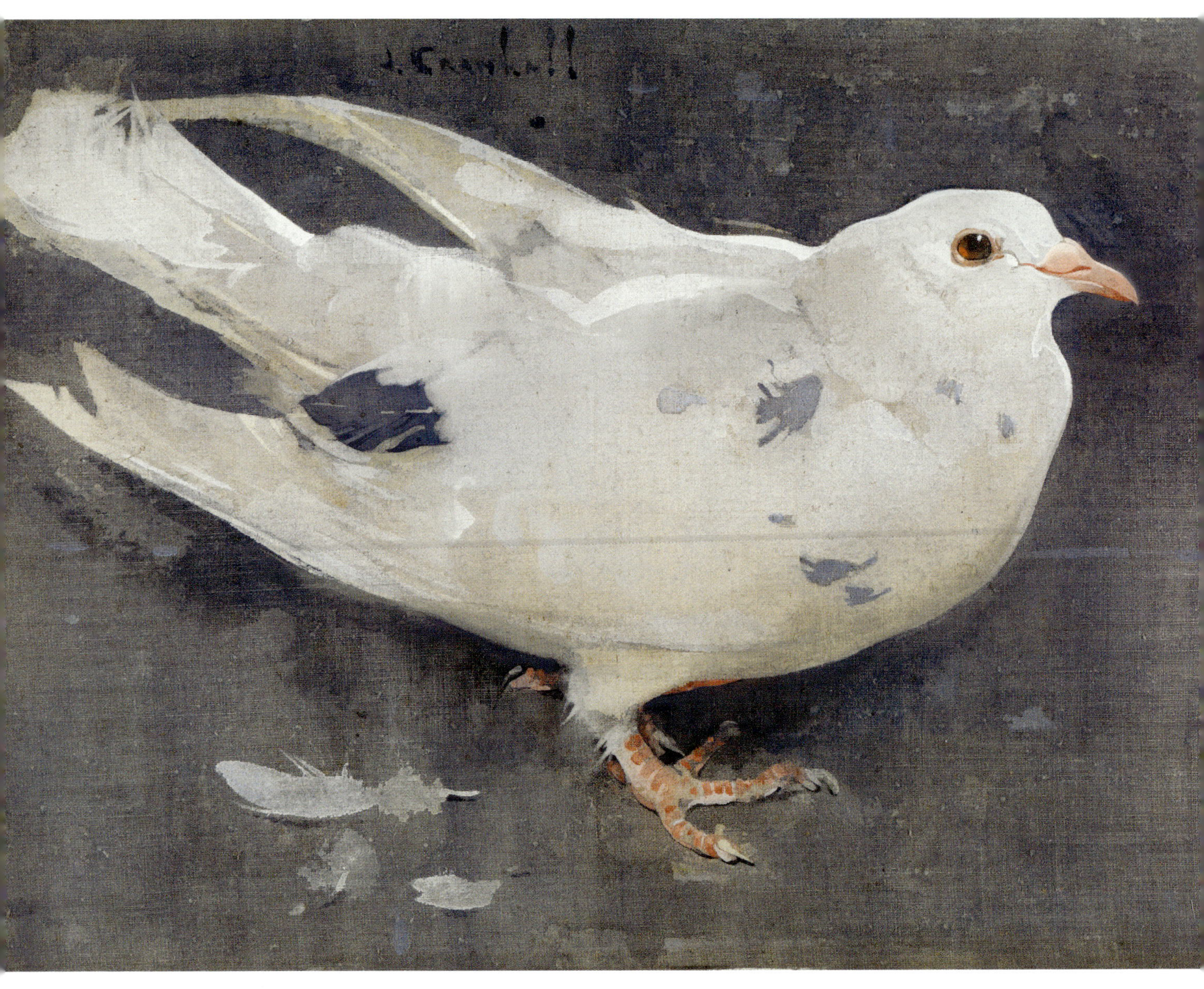

***The Pigeon,*** about 1894
Watercolour and bodycolour on linen
23.5 x 31.1 cm
35.172

This delicate study of a white pigeon shows, in the treatment of its amber eye and sharp scaly claw, the subtlety of Crawhall's characterization. The fallen feathers are no accidental accessory but essential to the overall compositional balance of this harmony in pink, white and grey.

# *Fur and Feathers*

Crawhall had a rapport not only with horses, but with all animals and birds. Indeed, many of his contemporaries commented that he seemed more at ease with animals than people. He would spend hours observing them, according to Cunninghame Graham, 'with a look so intense it seemed to burn a hole into their skin.' Then with a few strokes he would capture peculiarities of character and skilfully articulate feathers, fur and hide. Charles Keene jokingly described Crawhall in 1878 as a budding Edwin Landseer (1802–1873), then the most popular and successful British animal painter, patronized and knighted by Queen Victoria (1819–1901). However, Crawhall's style of animal painting was quite different to that of Landseer's romanticized and sentimental academy pieces.

Crawhall led the way in a new brand of animal depiction based on accumulated knowledge and the poetic distillation of character. His paintings are perceptive and expressive, conveying movement, individuality and substance with an epigrammatic precision, combined with a decorative concern for colour and the harmonious balance of line and form. His works are not portraits – he was not interested in commissions to paint specific prize-bred beasts or beloved household pets, as some artists were, although these would no doubt have been lucrative.

Neither did Crawhall desire to be an animal illustrator, despite having the instinctive ability with his acute observation, quick elegant lines and visual wit. He contributed illustrations to a number of his father's books, including *Border Notes and Mixty-Maxty* (1880), *The Compleatest Angling Booke that euer was writ* (1881) and *Olde ffrendes wyth newe Faces* (1883). He also provided drawings for the wildlife volume of his cousin Abel Chapman (1851–1929), *Unexplored Spain* (1910), the decadent literary periodical *The Yellow Book* and articles by his friends

Armour and Frías. However, Crawhall preferred not to be tied into the drudgery of a commercial illustrator, supplying weekly drawings to an editor, a position lamented by Keene. His correspondence with Reid shows that he was concerned about maintaining an income but, with an allowance from his family, he was in the privileged position of retaining autonomy over what he produced and when.

Crawhall's animal studies connected with Burrell and his family's interests. When living at Hutton Castle, they were surrounded by farmland and livestock, and kept horses, dogs, chickens and a parrot. Burrell became a patron of the Chirnside Poultry, Pigeons, Rabbits and Cage Birds Society and donated two cups to the Paxton Agricultural Show for the best horse and Aberdeen Angus.

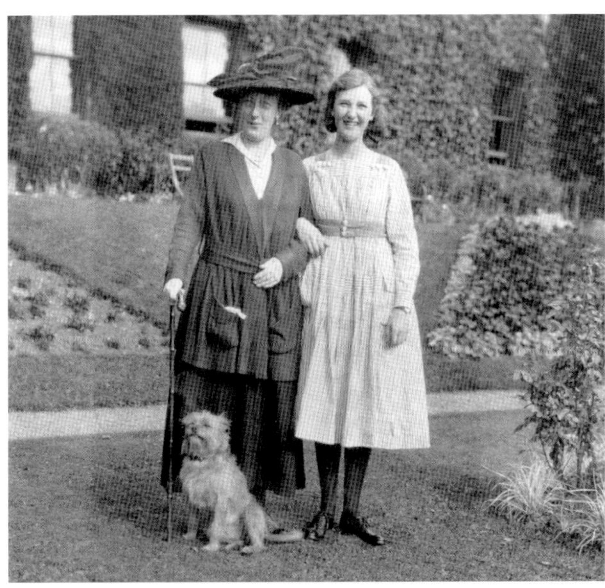

Constance Burrell and her daughter Marion, later Silvia (1902–92), with their terrier, Letham, in the gardens of Kilduff House in East Lothian, probably in the late 1910s. Collection of SMO Stephen.

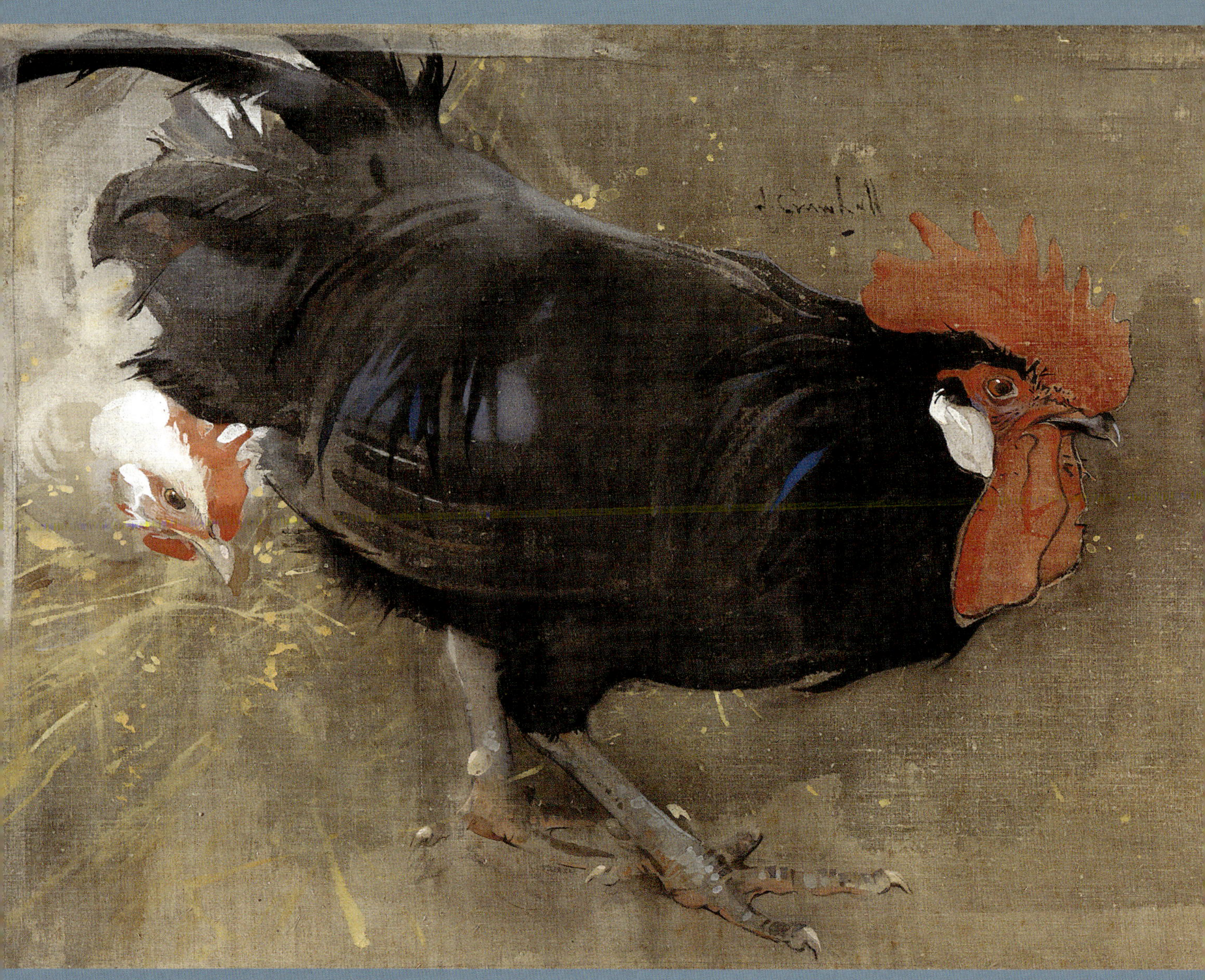

# Artwork in Focus

***The Black Cock,*** 1894
Watercolour and bodycolour on linen
39.5 x 51.2 cm
35.82

Crawhall returned again and again to painting cockerels, enjoying their bold colours, strutting attitude and extravagant display. They physically and suggestively dominate his compositions. In *The Black Cock* the male bird sidelines the white hen pecking at scattered straw behind him. However, it is she who sets off his glossy mantle of blue-black feathers and magnificent red comb and wattle, providing pictorial balance and unity. The straw from which she feeds creates a diagonal radius from which the cockerel confidently steps.

*The Black Cock* was praised by critics when it was shown at an exhibition of the International Society of Sculptors, Painters and Gravers in London in 1898, as epitomizing Crawhall's keen powers of observation and skill in capturing animal character and behaviour, allied with an intrinsic understanding of colour and design. It went on to win a silver medal at the Paris Exposition of 1900.

Burrell and his family enthusiastically lent their Crawhalls to local, national and international exhibitions. *The Black Cock* was lent by Burrell to Glasgow's 1901 International Exhibition along with *The Aviary, Clifton* (pp.16–17) and *The Pigeon* (p. 48). His brother George (1857–1927) lent *Black Rabbit* (about 1894; Paul Mellon Collection, Yale Center for British Art). Burrell was one of the key lenders to this exhibition and was also on the organizing committee.

*'wherein analysis and generalization are triumphantly combined'*

Frank Rinder, *Art Journal*, 1911

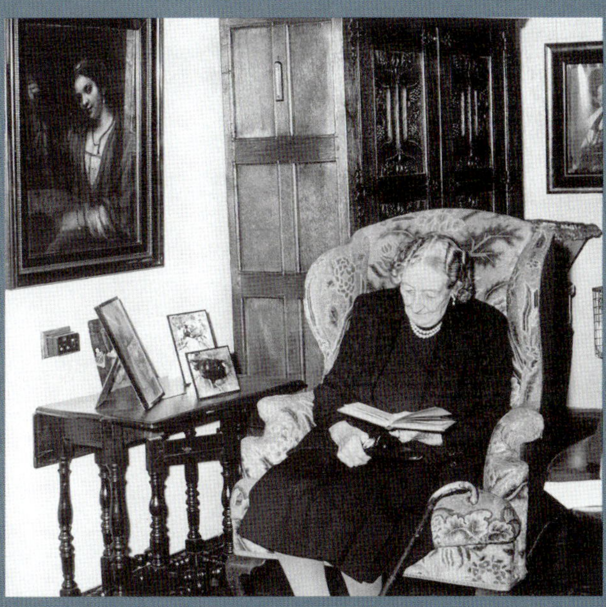

Constance, Lady Burrell in her sitting room at Hutton Castle around 1958–61. On the side table are framed reproductions of *The Black Cock* and *The Aviary, Clifton*. Family favourites, these were the artworks she chose to keep beside her in old age. Glasgow Museums Archive, GMA.2013.1.1.2464.

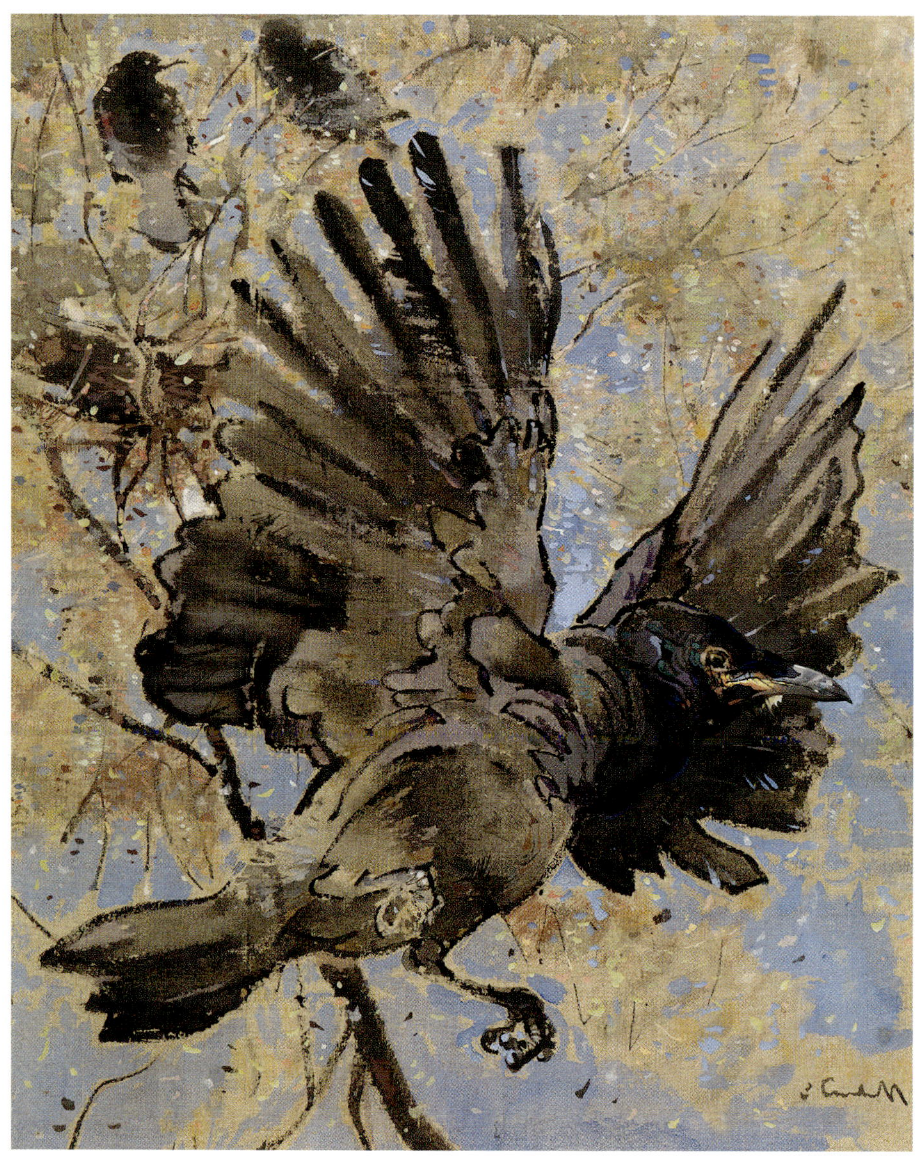

***The Rook's Nest,*** about 1908
Bodycolour on linen
55.9 x 43.2 cm
35.186

Among Crawhall's most outstanding works are those which capture a bird in flight. Here a juvenile rook has been disturbed from its roost. Its outstretched black wings convey its alarm. They fill the composition and contrast spectacularly with the bright blue sky behind. The bird's sharp glinting bill, intelligent eye, sharp-clawed feet and iridescent plumage, flecked with purple, pink and blue, are beautifully observed, all the more remarkable for having been painted from memory. The diagonal branch and dappled tree foliage create a decorative pattern behind the bird. Its nest and two other birds on the branches above perfectly balance the composition.

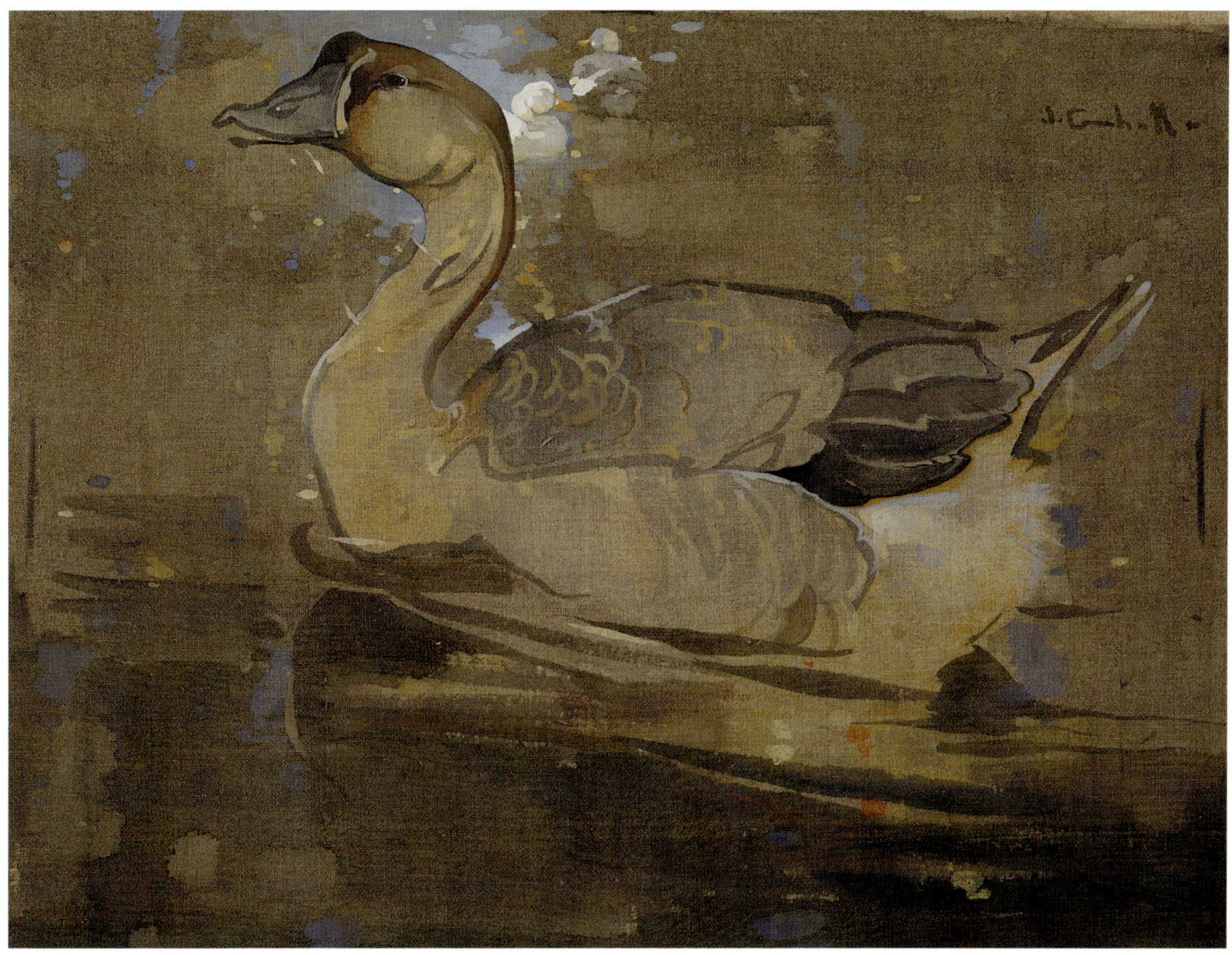

### *The Chinese Goose,* 1905
Bodycolour on linen
30.5 x 37.5 cm
35.98

Painted from memory, Crawhall's compositions were necessarily distilled and abbreviated. In this painting he catches the enquiring look of the goose, beak slightly parted, as it looks back towards the viewer, reflected blue sky haloing its head, its orange legs faintly suggested beneath the ripples. Light, filtered through the trees, stipples the water and highlights

the bird's upturned tail feathers and downy behind. With the barest of means Crawhall creates an entire setting, two white ducks in the background and the reflections of tall trees around them. The linen is used to set the tone and define the body of the goose.

*The Chinese Goose* was one of six artworks Crawhall selected for exhibition in London in the summer of 1909 at the New English Art Club, of which he had just become a member. He exhibited a further four works at the club's winter exhibition that year.

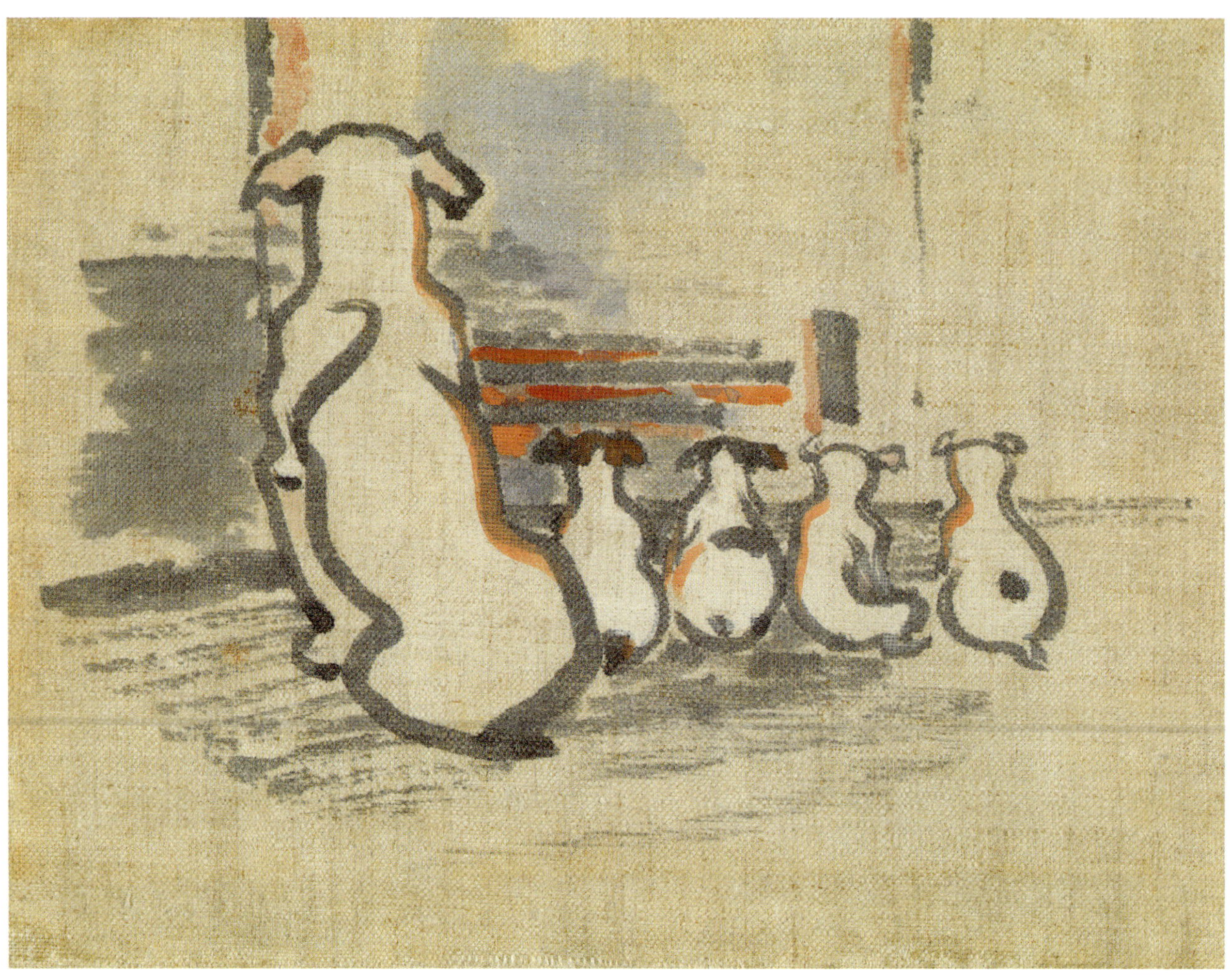

***Foxhound and Puppies,*** about 1903
Bodycolour on linen
12.1 x 15.3 cm
35.118

Although very simple in construction, this sketch shows remarkable artistry and perception, demonstrating Crawhall's illustrative ability. A foxhound sits by the hearth with her four puppies ranged in a row. Orange highlights on their shoulders and rumps suggest the reflected warmth of the fire. The sinuous curves of their bodies are balanced by the horizontal lines of the grate through which the glow of the fire can be seen and at which the puppies stare fixedly, ears raised and alert. This modest but endearing image is a strong piece of observational design.

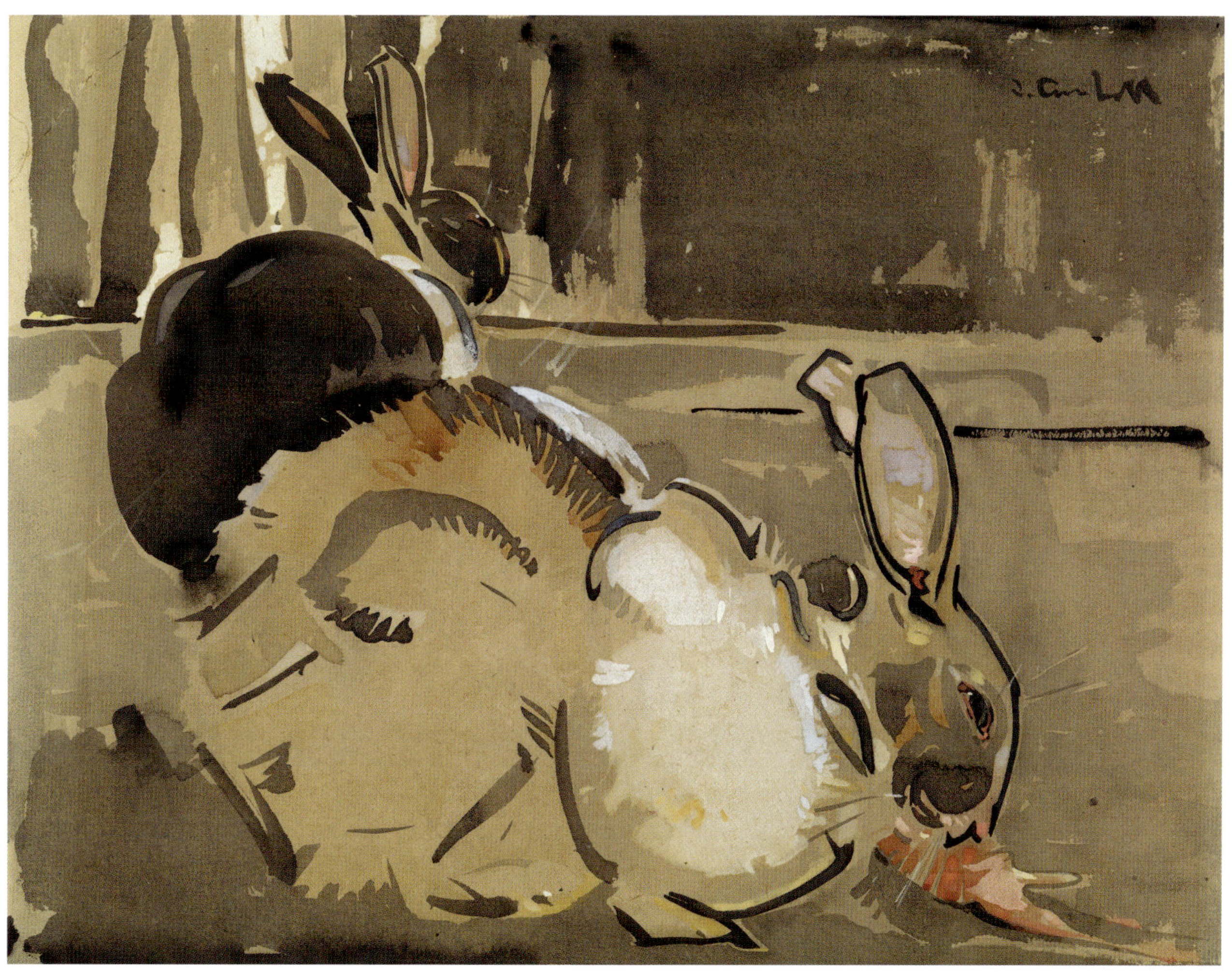

**_Two Rabbits, One Eating Carrots,_** about 1893
Wash and bodycolour on paper
29.5 x 37.4 cm
35.199

One rabbit in profile, one in three-quarter view from behind, this drawing is simply delineated but captures the characteristic behaviour of these family favourites. Back legs bunched up, one gently nibbles a carrot. Delicate touches of white, pink and blue bodycolour define insides of alert ears and questioning nose, and suggest light falling on soft fur. Writing in the _Art Journal_ in 1911, Scottish art critic Frank Rinder (1863–1937) compared Crawhall's more finished _Black Rabbit_ (see p. 51) to _Young Hare_ (1502; Albertina, Vienna), a watercolour by German Renaissance painter Albrecht Dürer (1471–1528), famous for its accuracy of observation. This drawing, although sketch-like, also displays that impressive incisiveness.

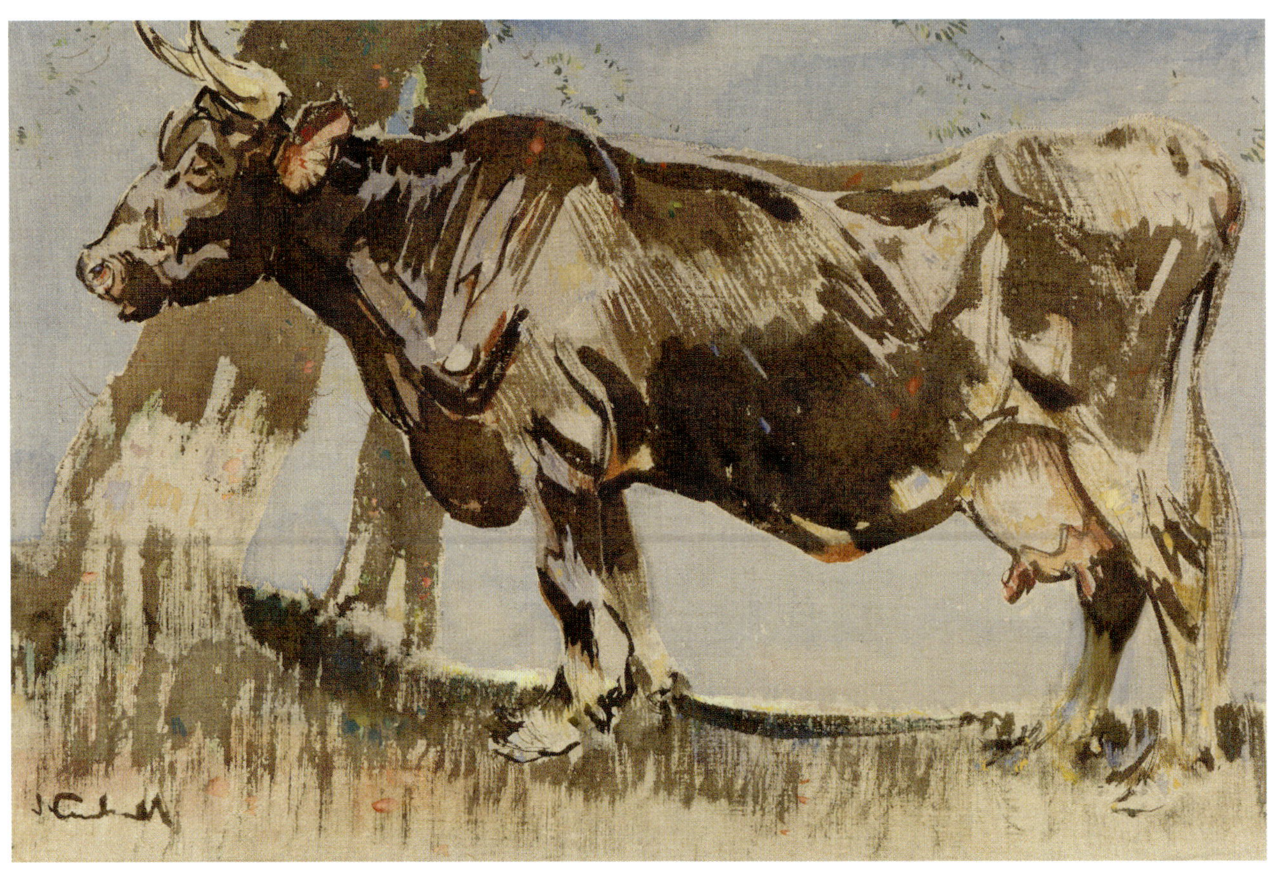

**_The Old Cow,_** about 1894–1903
Watercolour and bodycolour on linen
30.5 x 45.7 cm
35.167

This watercolour is reminiscent of Crawhall's childhood drawing after Thomas Bewick's *The Chillingham Bull*, showing a bull in profile in a landscape setting (p. 8). Yet it demonstrates how far Crawhall had come since those early days of exact copying. The marks Crawhall makes are selective and decorative, barely defining form, creating a flat pattern of colour and line set against an abstracted blue background. Nevertheless, he still manages to sensitively convey the gaunt flanks, sagging flesh, worn udders and curled overgrown hooves of this weary elderly animal left out to pasture.

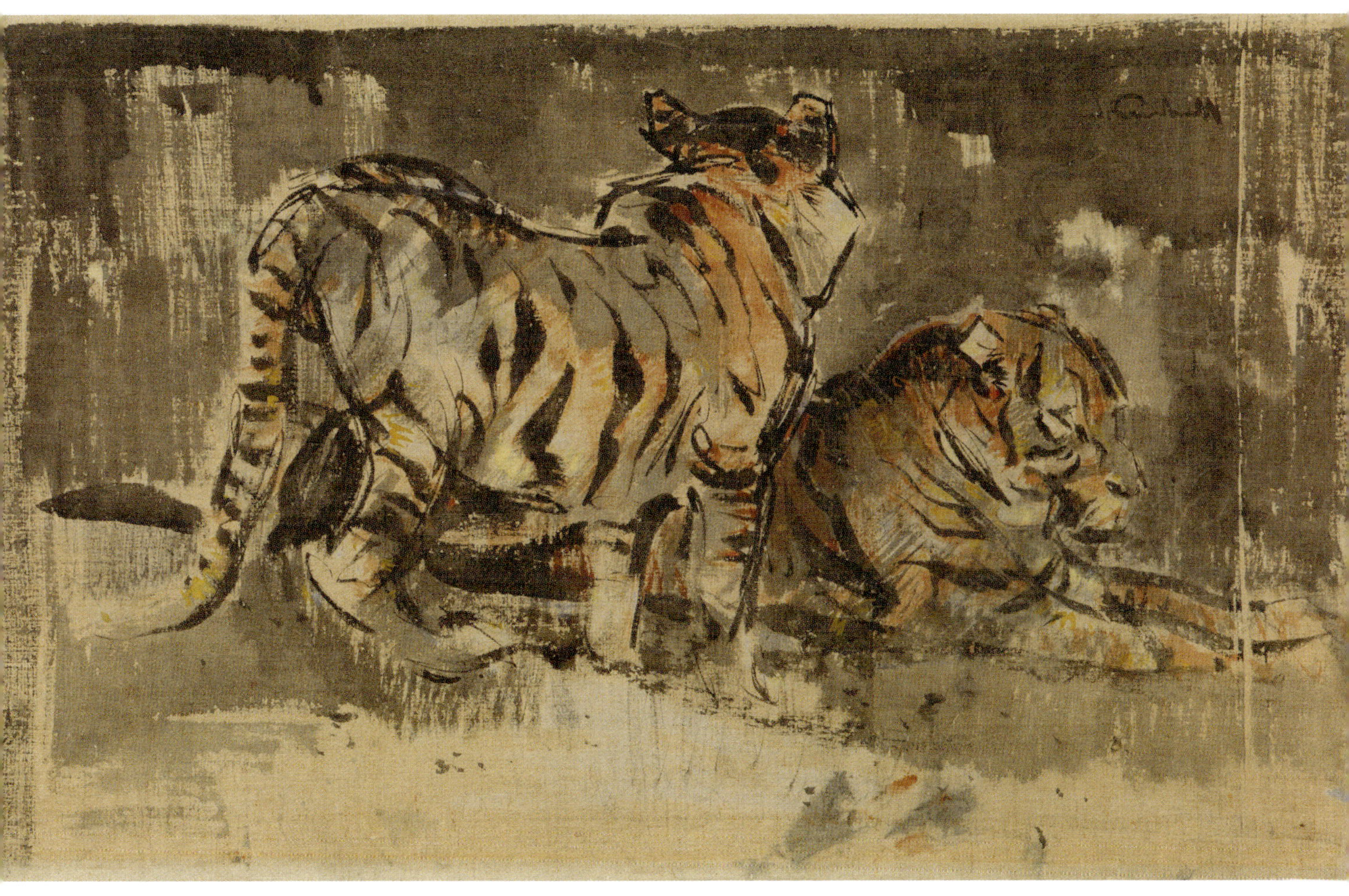

**Tigers,** about 1894–98
Bodycolour on linen
37.5 x 60.4 cm
35.194

In the 1890s London Zoo in Regent's Park was a favourite destination for many animal painters. Crawhall's depiction of two sleepy tigers may well have been inspired by a visit there. Tigers were kept inside at London Zoo until 1902 because of fears they would succumb to the cold. Crawhall drew tigers on a number of occasions, usually placing them within an imagined savannah setting and suggesting something of the power and ferocity of their natures. However, here he makes no attempt to portray anything other than a bleak enclosure containing two bored, unstimulated big cats.

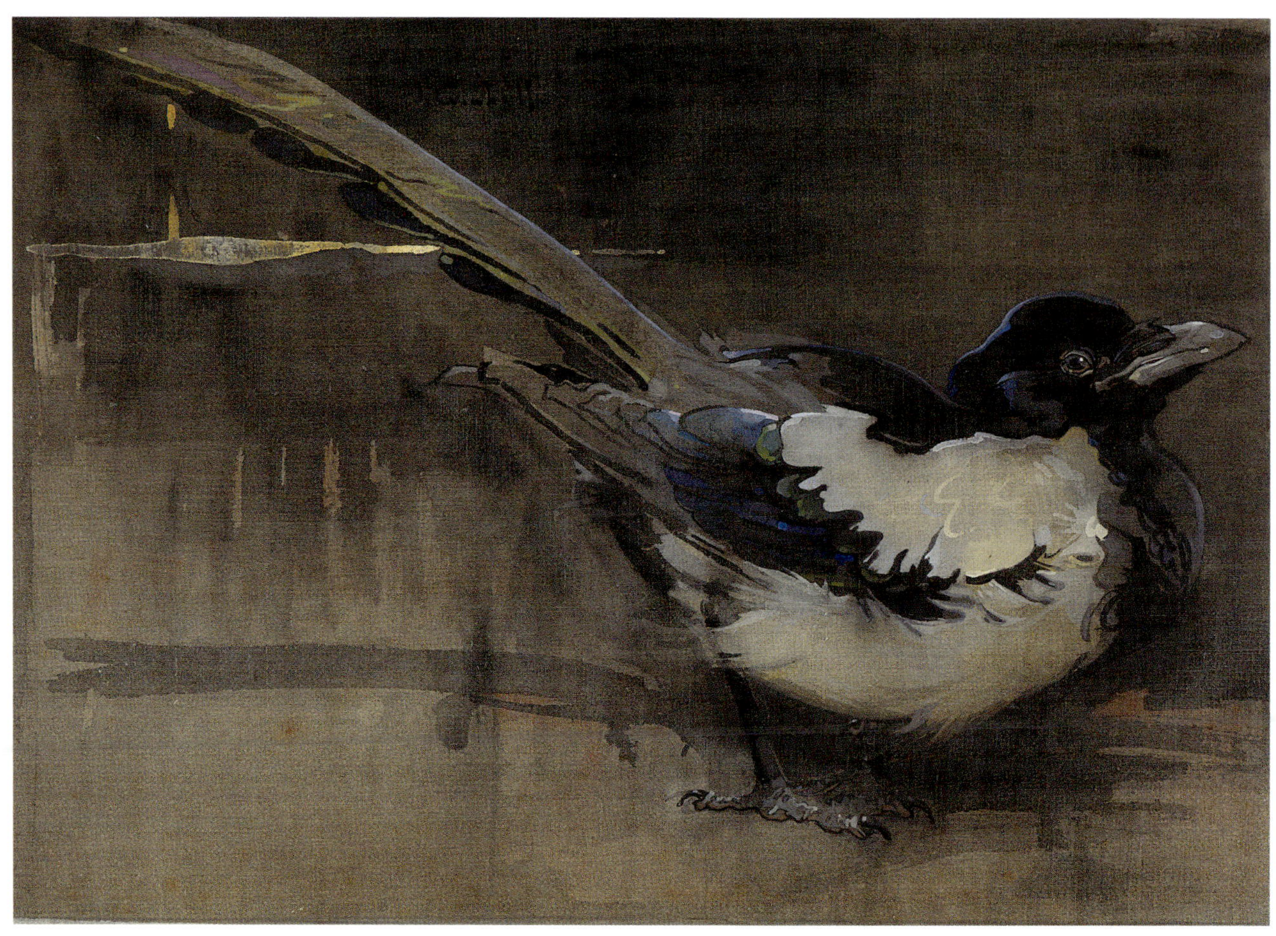

***The Magpie,*** about 1906
Watercolour and bodycolour on linen
29.3 x 43.2 cm
35.151

Burrell's major competitor when it came to collecting Crawhall watercolours was Paisley industrialist WA Coats. He owned 46 works, including this watercolour of a quizzical magpie, in which light catches the iridescent sheen of feathers and the gleam of sharp beak and intelligent eye. Burrell bought it, along with two others, in January 1927 at an exhibition of Coats' Crawhall collection, organized by WB Paterson at the Royal Society of British Artists, in London. Burrell bought a further eleven works through Reid & Lefevre from the sale of Coats' collection at Christie's on 12 April 1935.

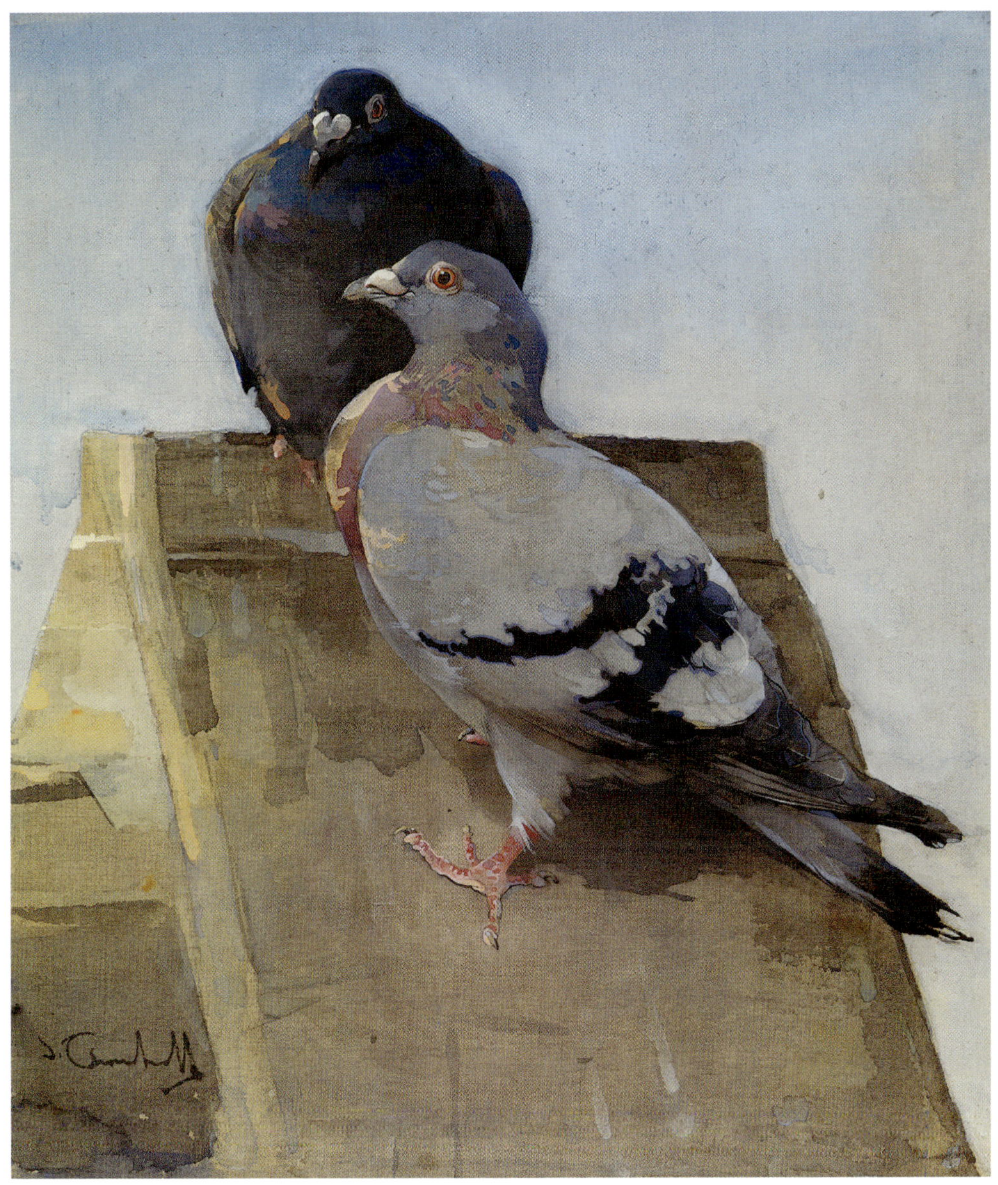

**Pigeons on the Roof,** about 1895
Bodycolour on linen
38.1 x 32.4 cm
35.173

Other important Glasgow collectors of Crawhall's work included the shipbroker and insurance agent Leonard Gow (1859–1936), oil magnate David William Traill Cargill (1872–1939) and stockbroker John Augustus Holms (1866–1938). Holms bought *Pigeons on the Roof* from Reid in October 1904 for £110. Burrell acquired it on 17 June 1932 from Reid & Lefevre for £330, three times the price Holms had paid, but he insured it for £750, indicating his view of its true market value. Prices soared after the artist's death in 1913. Burrell's increased lending in the 1930s, when he began thinking of donating his collection to the public, helped keep insurance values high.

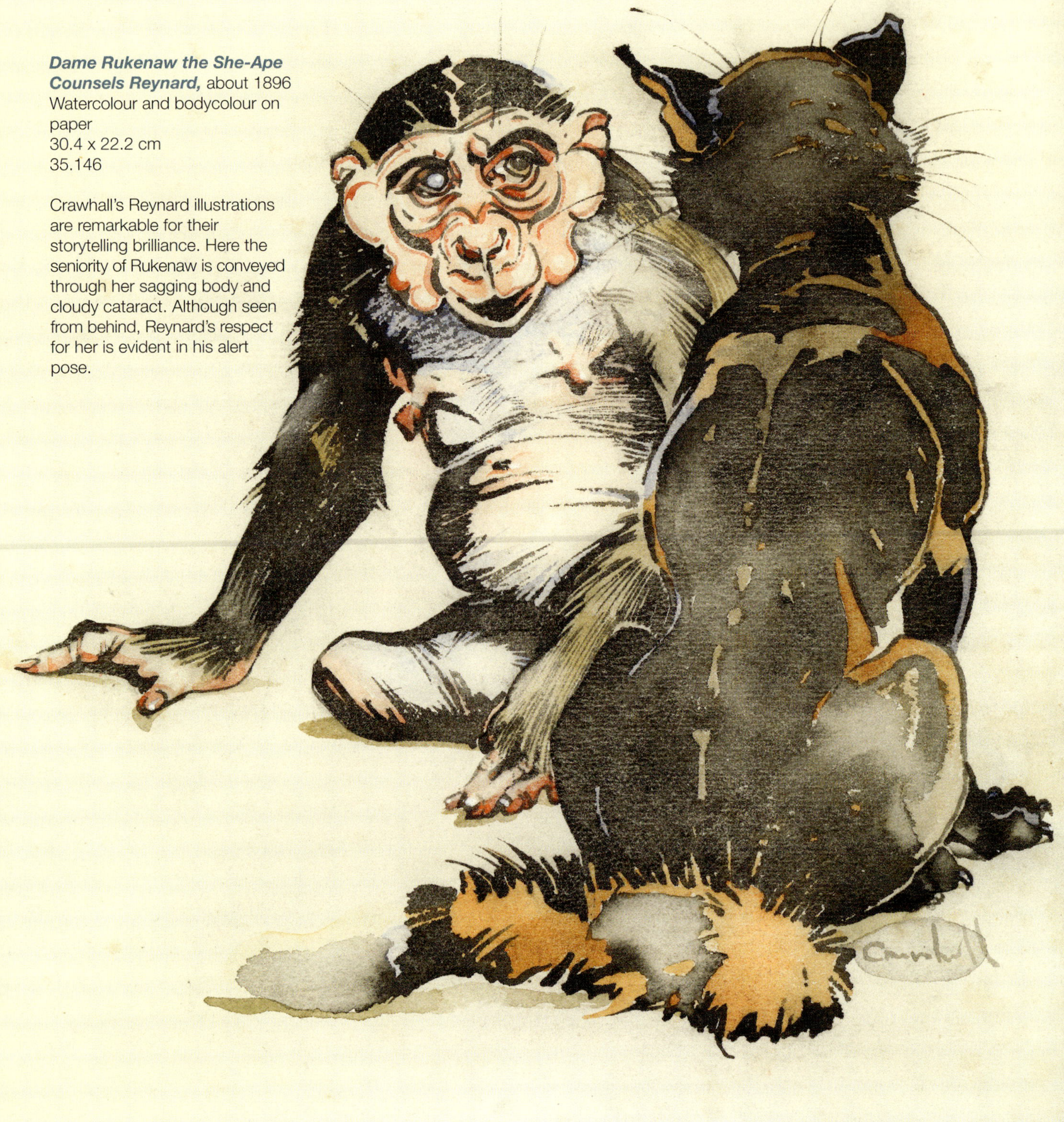

***Dame Rukenaw the She-Ape
Counsels Reynard,*** about 1896
Watercolour and bodycolour on
paper
30.4 x 22.2 cm
35.146

Crawhall's Reynard illustrations
are remarkable for their
storytelling brilliance. Here the
seniority of Rukenaw is conveyed
through her sagging body and
cloudy cataract. Although seen
from behind, Reynard's respect
for her is evident in his alert
pose.

# Reynard the Fox

In 1896 Crawhall made 10 watercolour illustrations of the medieval fable of Reynard the Fox for Glasgow textile manufacturer Thomas Glen Arthur (1857–1907). They were intended to be bound into a copy of *The History of Reynard the Fox* that Arthur owned, possibly a facsimile edition of William Caxton's 1481 translation from Dutch, on which Crawhall's drawings appear to be based. There were many versions of the story, in Latin, French, German and Dutch, the earliest dating from the twelfth century. Narrating the tricks that the wily Reynard plays on unsuspecting individuals within the animal kingdom, the tales were as popular as Aesop's animal-based fables. Their vulpine subject matter would have appealed to Arthur, who was a keen huntsman and a member of the Eglinton and Renfrew Hunt, with a stud stable at Carrick.

Some of the scenes that Crawhall chose to illustrate are the same as those selected in traditional woodcut cycles. However, Crawhall's approach was markedly original and modern, drawn from his observed knowledge of animal behaviour and Japanese prints. Crawhall's series had an immediate precedent in an 1895 edition of Reynard illustrated by Frank Calderon (1865–1943). Calderon's artwork was more conventionally descriptive, and a comparison of the two series demonstrates Crawhall's innovation.

Crawhall's drawings were made at Brockenhurst in Hampshire where he was staying with his sister Judith following the death of their father in 1896. The financial uncertainty for the family around this time perhaps helps to explain this unusual commission, as illustrative work was not Crawhall's natural preference. The animal focus of the illustrations would certainly have appealed to him and the series may have been undertaken as a personal tribute to his father, who had published many such traditional tales, illustrated by himself and, on occasion, by Crawhall.

In the end Arthur decided not to bind the drawings into his Reynard edition, possibly due to his failing health, and sold them instead to the dealer WB Paterson. Arthur's brother-in-law WA Coats bought them from Paterson around 1906, giving Paterson permission to publish a limited edition of 200 copies at 10 guineas each. After Coats' death, the original drawings passed to his sons, Thomas Heywood Coats of Nitshill (1889–1958) and Major John A Coats of Dundonald (1892–1932). Burrell seems to have had his eye on the set for some time and finally acquired it on 12 April 1935 from Christie's, London, through Reid & Lefevre, for a mere £336.

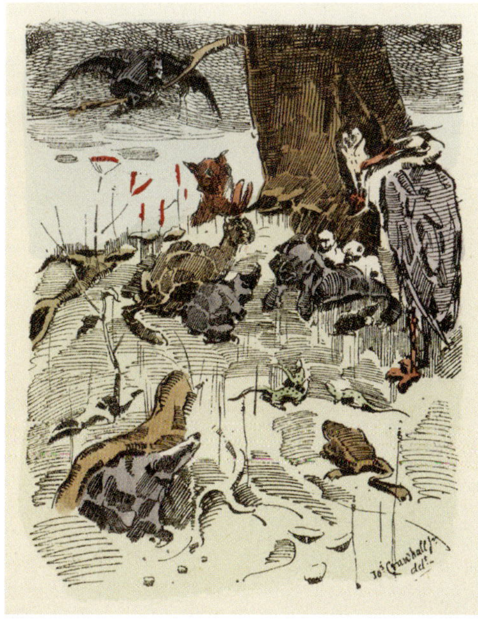

Crawhall's illustration to 'The Gloamin' buchte', a Border ballad published by his father, shows a variety of creatures, including a fox, congregating to listen to fairy song, a fascinating precursor to his Reynard the Fox series. *Olde ffrendes wyth newe Faces*, by Joseph Crawhall snr, 1883. Glasgow Museums Archive, GMA.2013.1.6.852.

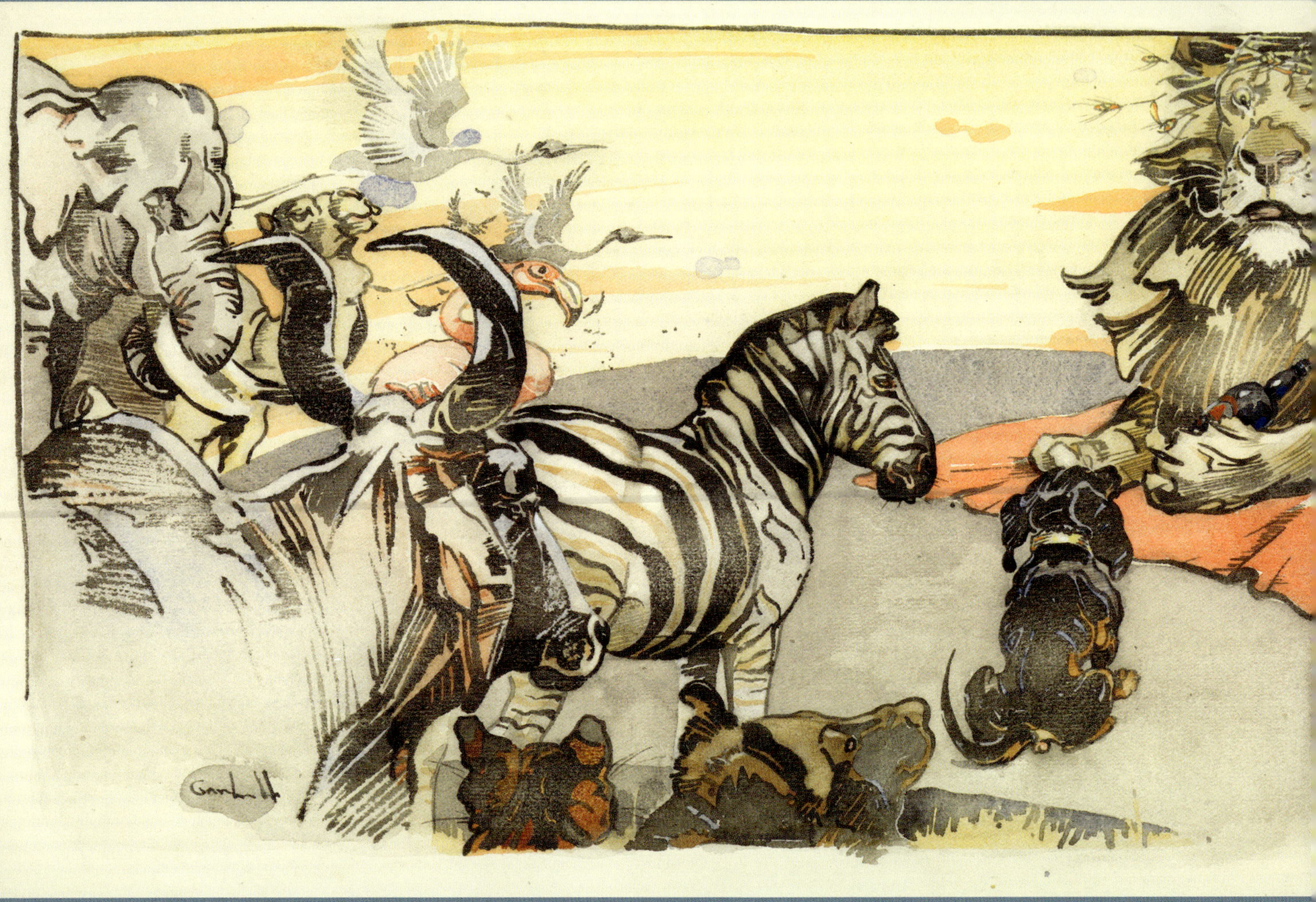

# Artwork in Focus



***Curtois the Hound at Noble's Court,***
about 1896
Watercolour on paper
25.5 x 31.2 cm
35.148

This scene showing all the animals assembled at Noble the Lion's court is the traditional opening to the sequence of tales about the exploits of Reynard the Fox. The king sits on a red rug, facing the viewer. Reynard is the only animal who fails to appear because he knows the others are angry with him. One by one the animals come forward to report Reynard's crimes. Crawhall shows Curtois the Hound complaining that in the winter when he was cold and hungry Reynard stole his food.

Like Calderon, Crawhall embellishes the story, introducing a wide variety of creatures including a zebra, buffalo, bear, wolf, zebu, camel, elephant, flamingo and flying storks. However, Crawhall's king wears an African woven grass crown and sits like a lion, not a western official, albeit Crawhall humorously has him clutch a bottle of beer. Both artists arrange the animal petitioners with their backs to the viewer, facing the king, making the viewer feel they are part of the court gathering, but Crawhall crops heads and bodies, giving his scene greater immediacy. The beauty, balance and restraint of Crawhall's diagonal composition is much more avant-garde, inspired by the pictorial construction of Japanese prints.

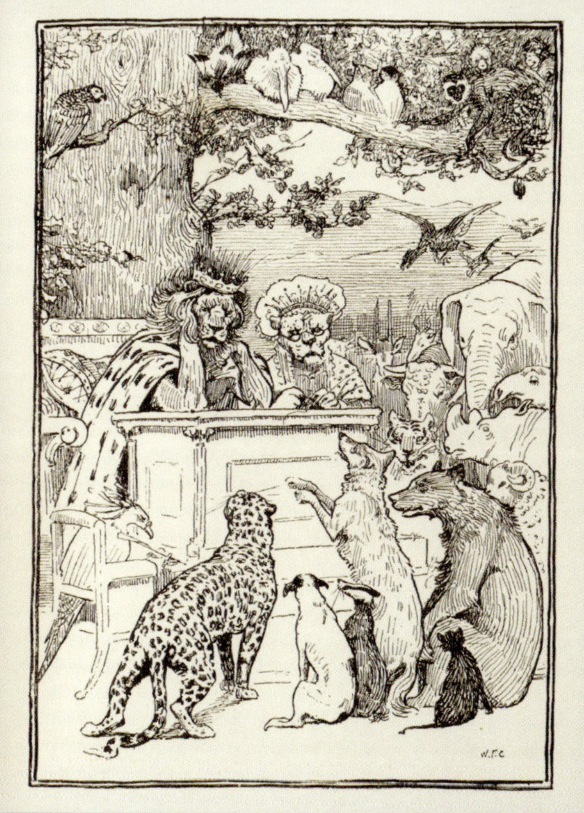

Calderon's imagining of Noble the Lion's' court is a very sedate, Victorian affair. Anthropomorphized, those in power sit in chairs at a desk wearing ceremonial robes, crowns and even spectacles as they listen to complainants. *The Court of King Noble* by Frank Calderon, frontispiece to *The Most Delectable History of Reynard the Fox*, ed. Joseph Jacobs, 1895.

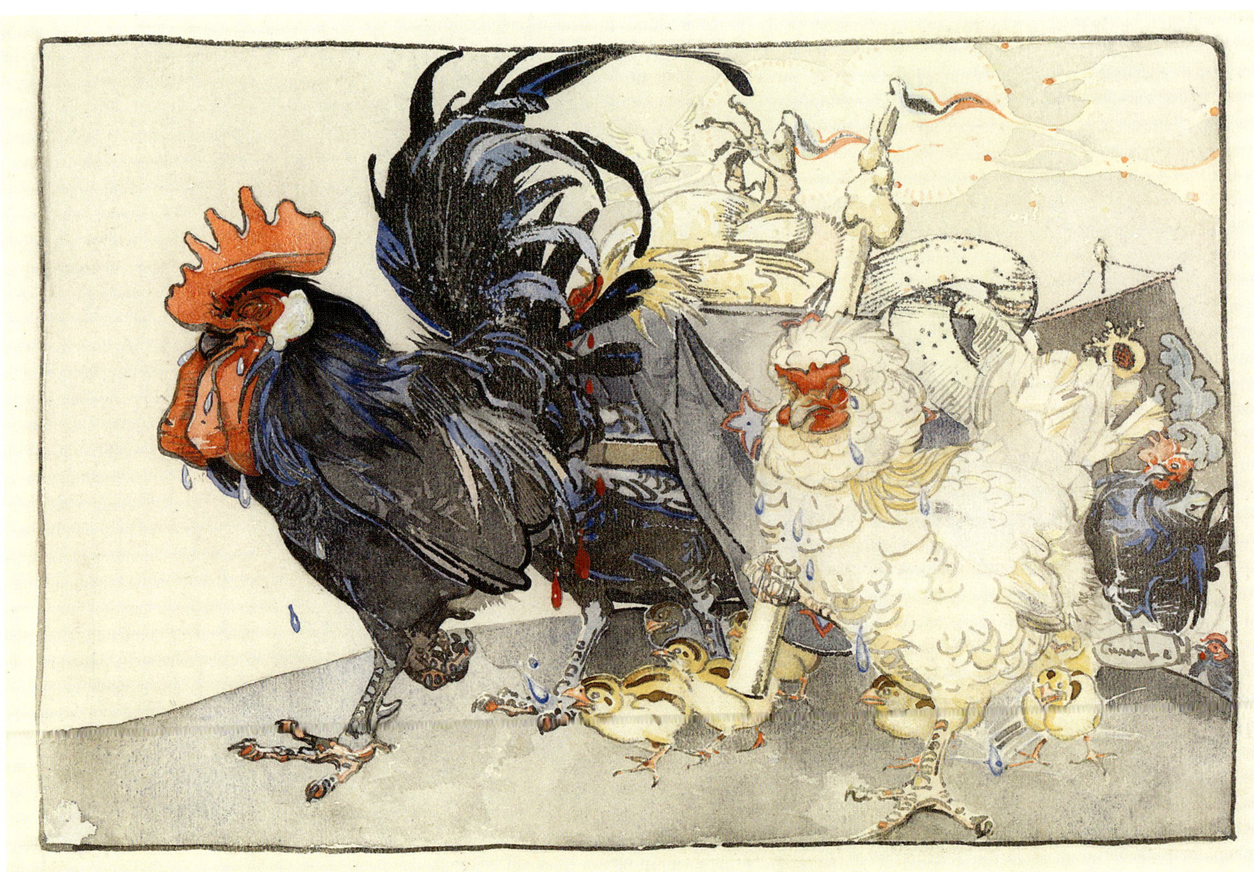

**Chanticleer and the Funeral Procession of Coppen,** about 1896
Watercolour on paper
25.3 x 31.6 cm
35.96

Reynard the Fox has killed Chanticleer the Cock's daughter Coppen, Reynard's eleventh victim from among the cockerel's fifteen daughters. Crawhall depicts the funeral procession, with Chanticleer taking the lead, followed by the chicks of Coppen and her surviving sisters Cantart and Crayant, carrying burning tapers. All are weeping. Coppen lies on her back on a bier, legs in the air, blood dripping from her severed neck. Blood mingles with tears. Crawhall's arrangement of birds and funerary paraphernalia deliberately creates visual confusion, the claustrophobic composition conveying the emotional turmoil and grief of the scene.

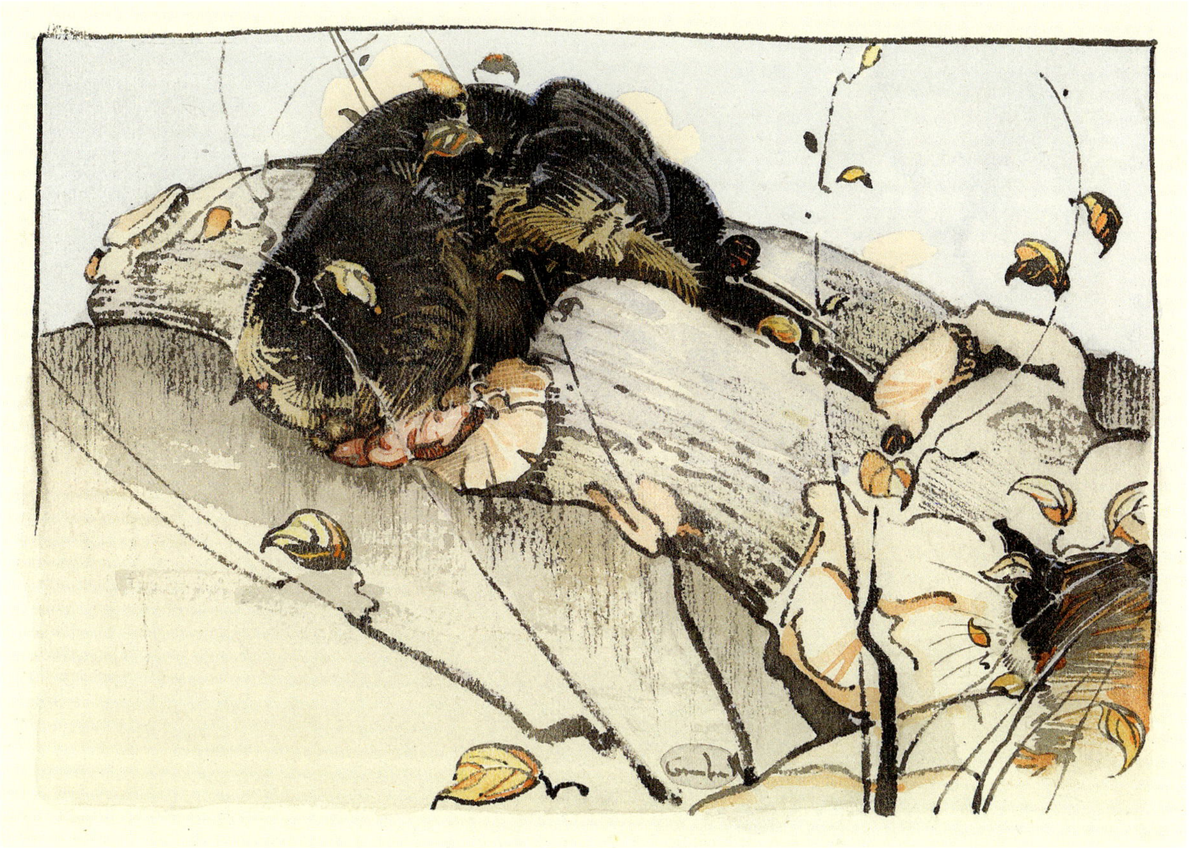

### How Bruin the Bear Ate the Honey,
about 1896
Watercolour and bodycolour on paper
24.4 x 30.6 cm
35.84

Bruin the Bear travels to Reynard's home in Malepardus
to summon him to court for punishment. Reynard
tricks Bruin into searching for honey within a felled oak
tree in the woodsman Lanfert's yard. He then removes
the wedges holding the split trunk open, trapping the
bear. Crawhall's composition is a direct visual quotation
from Calderon. However, Crawhall omits the frightened
villagers with their makeshift weapons and concentrates
on the predicament of the bear with Reynard watching
on. Removing the wider action, Crawhall transforms
the composition, focusing on the design aesthetics; the
strong diagonal emphasis and decorative foliage are
again influenced by Japanese prints.

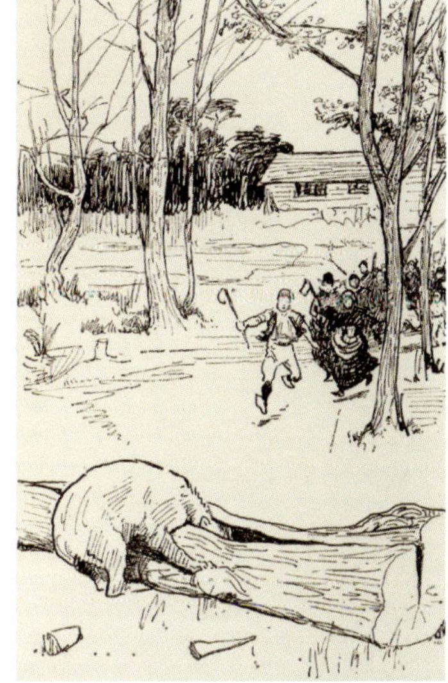

Frank Calderon
illustration to 'How
Bruin the Bear sped
with Reynard the Fox'
in *The Most Delectable
History of Reynard
the Fox*, ed. Joseph
Jacobs, 1895.

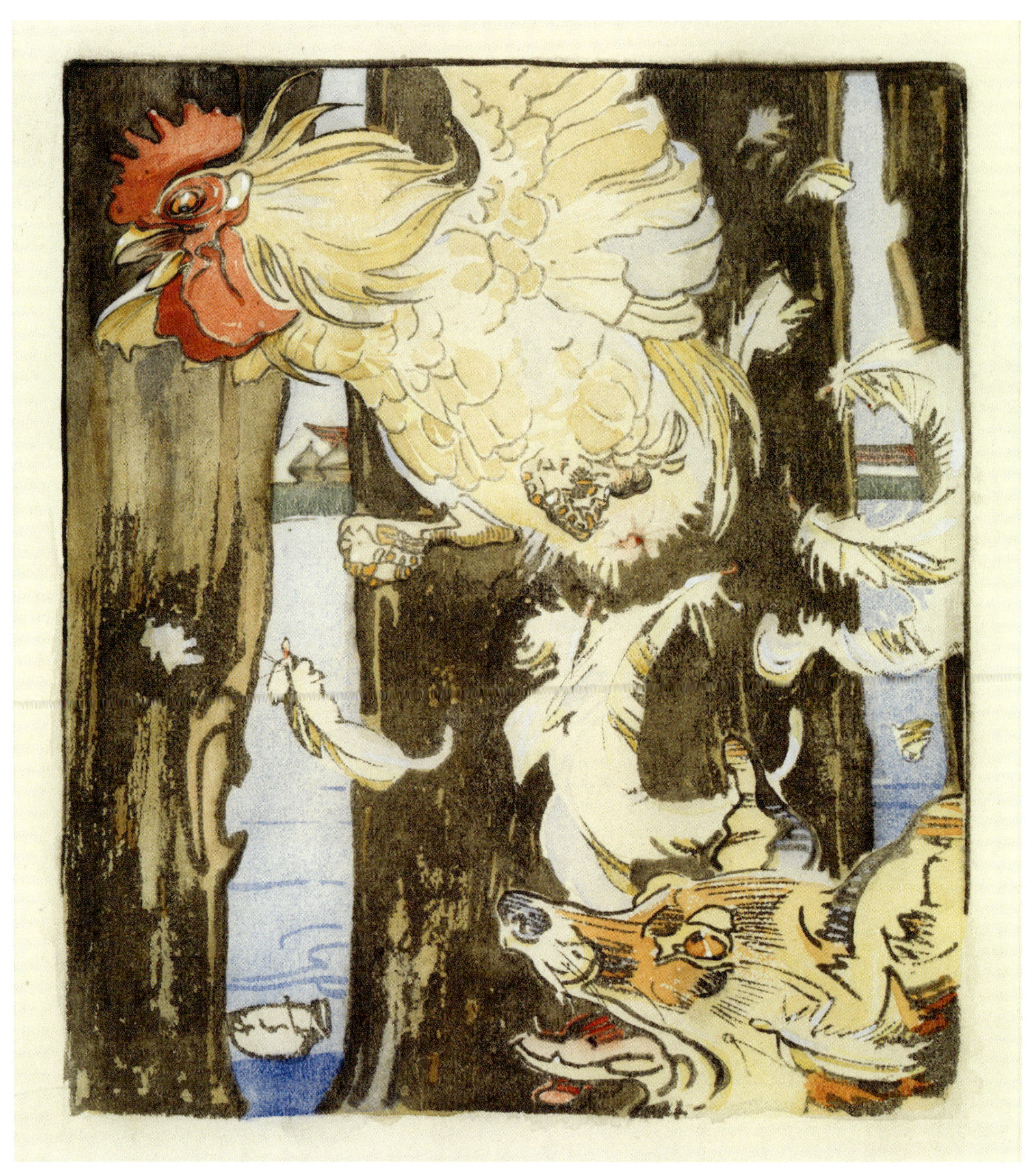

**_Cock Escaping from Reynard,_** about 1896
Watercolour on paper
30 x 24 cm
35.184

In a flurry of feathers a cockerel narrowly escapes the jaws of Reynard. The fox had promised to reform his behaviour and, persuaded by Grimbert the Badger, was on his way to attend Noble's court. However, seeing a group of hens and cockerels outside a convent, he could not resist pursuing a particularly plump male bird. Through the rotten, irregular planks of wood, Crawhall suggests the lack of protection offered to the fowl and gives a glimpse of farm buildings and a pond beyond, enlivening the composition with vertical bands of vivid blue. The whole composition is dynamic and concise.

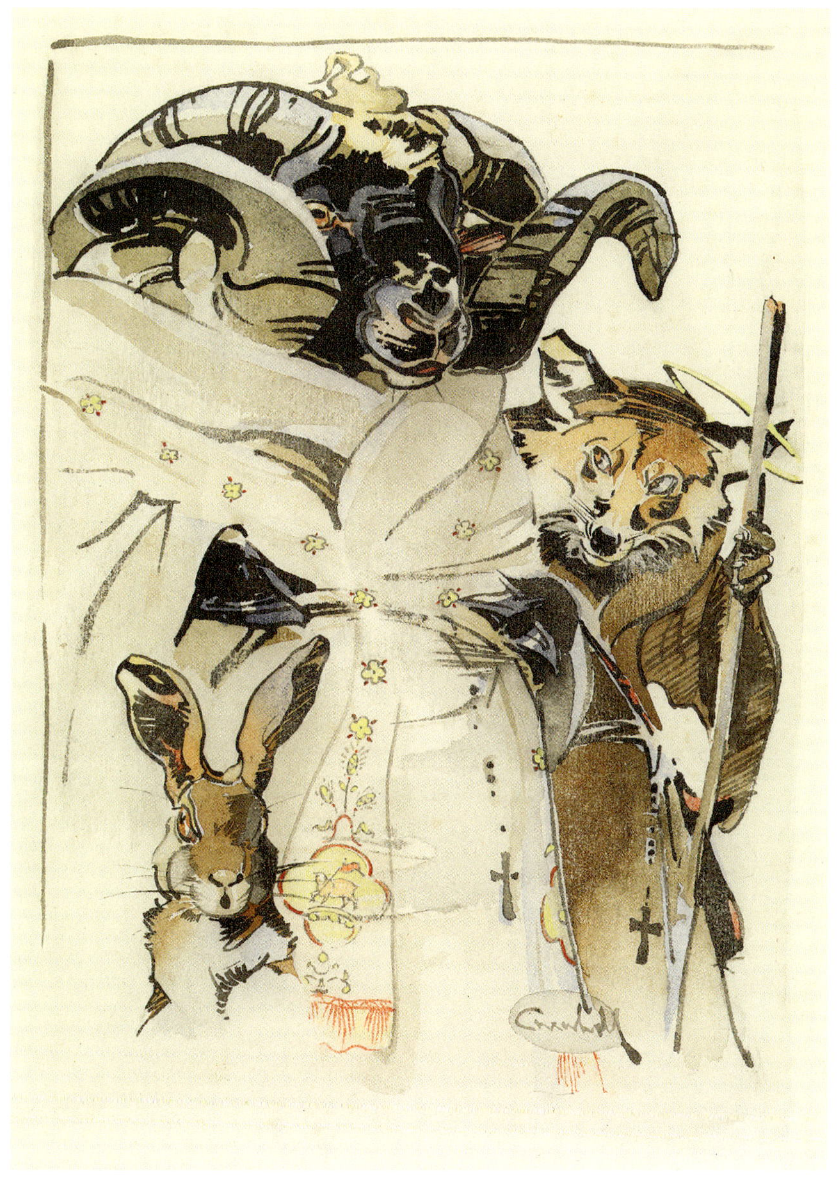

***Bellin the Ram, Cuwart the Hare and
Reynard the Fox,*** about 1896
Watercolour and bodycolour on paper
30.8 x 21.5 cm
35.81

At court Reynard only just avoids the death
sentence. In penance, he sets out on pilgrimage,
wearing a monk's habit, with a crucifix suspended
from his belt, and carrying a bag and staff. He asks
Bellin the Ram to bless him and join him for the start
of his journey, along with Cuwart the Hare. Crawhall
suggests Bellin the Ram's puffed up pride through
his ornate robes and Reynard's cunning with his
shifty glance. Humour is added through the ironic
and rather lopsided halo above Reynard's head.
Reynard has not changed. Cuwart, whose position
at the front is vulnerable, is soon dead.

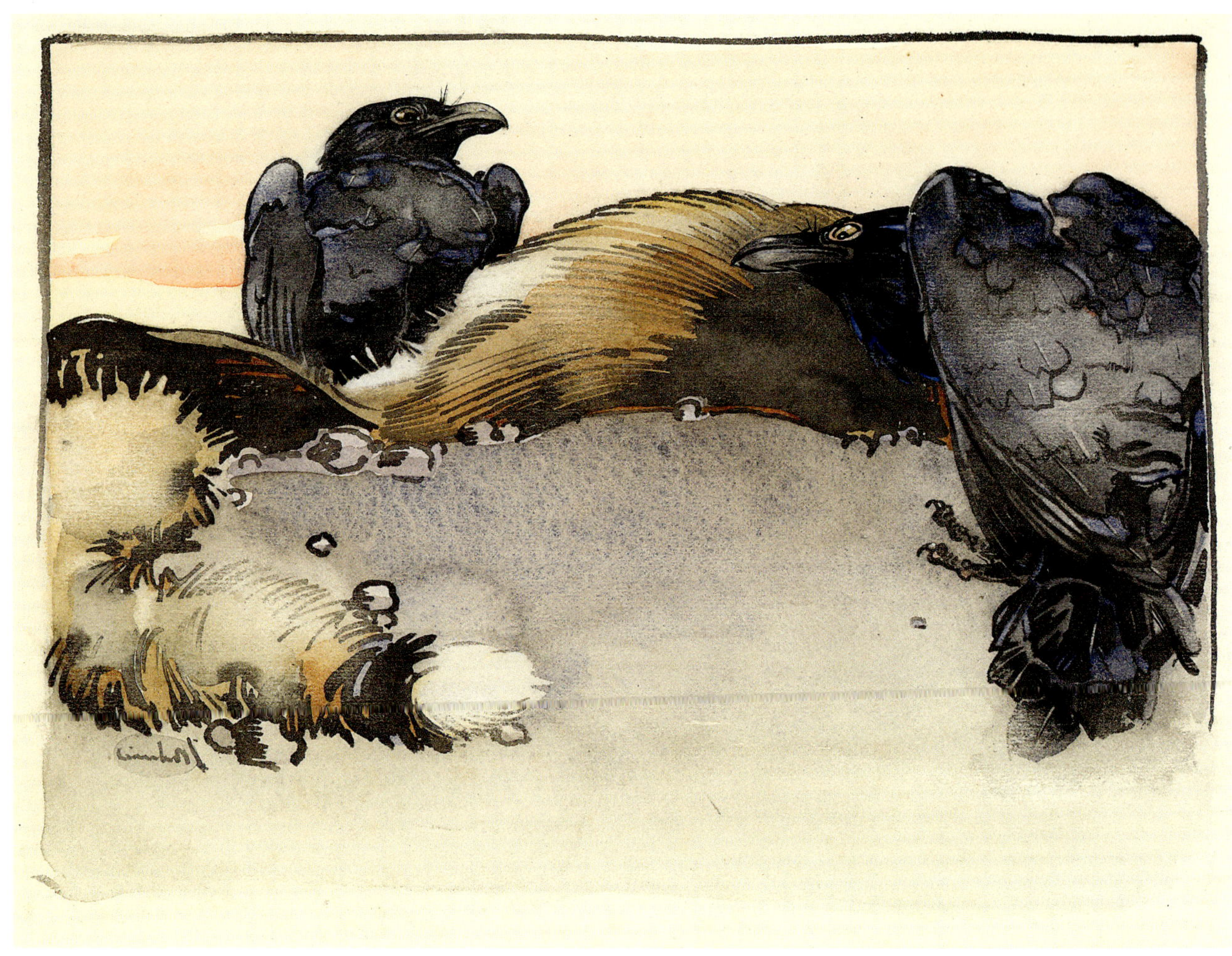

**Corbant the Rook and Reynard,** about 1896
Watercolour on paper
24 x 31 cm
35.95

Feigning death, Reynard is inspected by Corbant the Rook and his wife Sharpbeak. Showing only Reynard's belly and brush tail, Crawhall visually enhances the suggestion of a lifeless corpse. The rooks peer as they calculate the situation, Corbant silhouetted against the orange-pink sky and Sharpbeak hunched as she cocks her head to listen for the fox's breathing. The rich blue-black of their feathers contrasts with the warm red-brown of Reynard's coat. The moment is full of tension, as Reynard is about to spring to life and bite off Sharpbeak's head. Corbant, who escapes up a nearby tree, reports the attack to Noble the Lion.

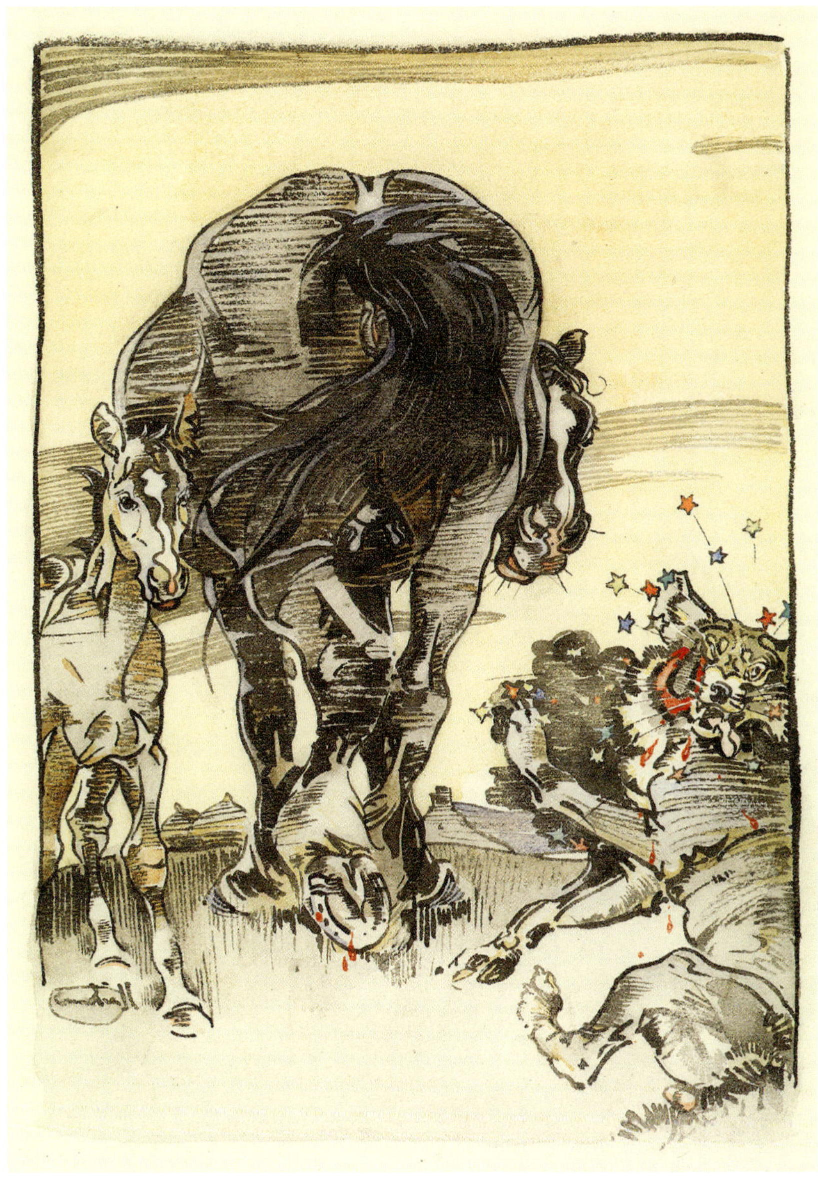

***Isegrim the Wolf and the Mare,*** about 1896
Watercolour and bodycolour on paper
30.9 x 24 cm
35.153

A mare swishes her tail in disdain, blood dripping
from her hoof, as she looks back at Isegrim the
Wolf lying dazed on the ground. Ravenously hungry,
Isegrim had asked Reynard to enquire if the mare
would sell her foal. She tells the fox that the terms
of sale are written on her hoof. Wisely, Reynard
claims illiteracy but the foolish wolf boasts he can
read many languages. The horse, recently reshod
with new iron shoes, kicks Isegrim on the head.
The low vantage point and rear view emphasizes
the mare's formidable haunches. Crawhall lightens
the mood, adding a hoof imprint on Isegrim's cheek
and stars around his head.

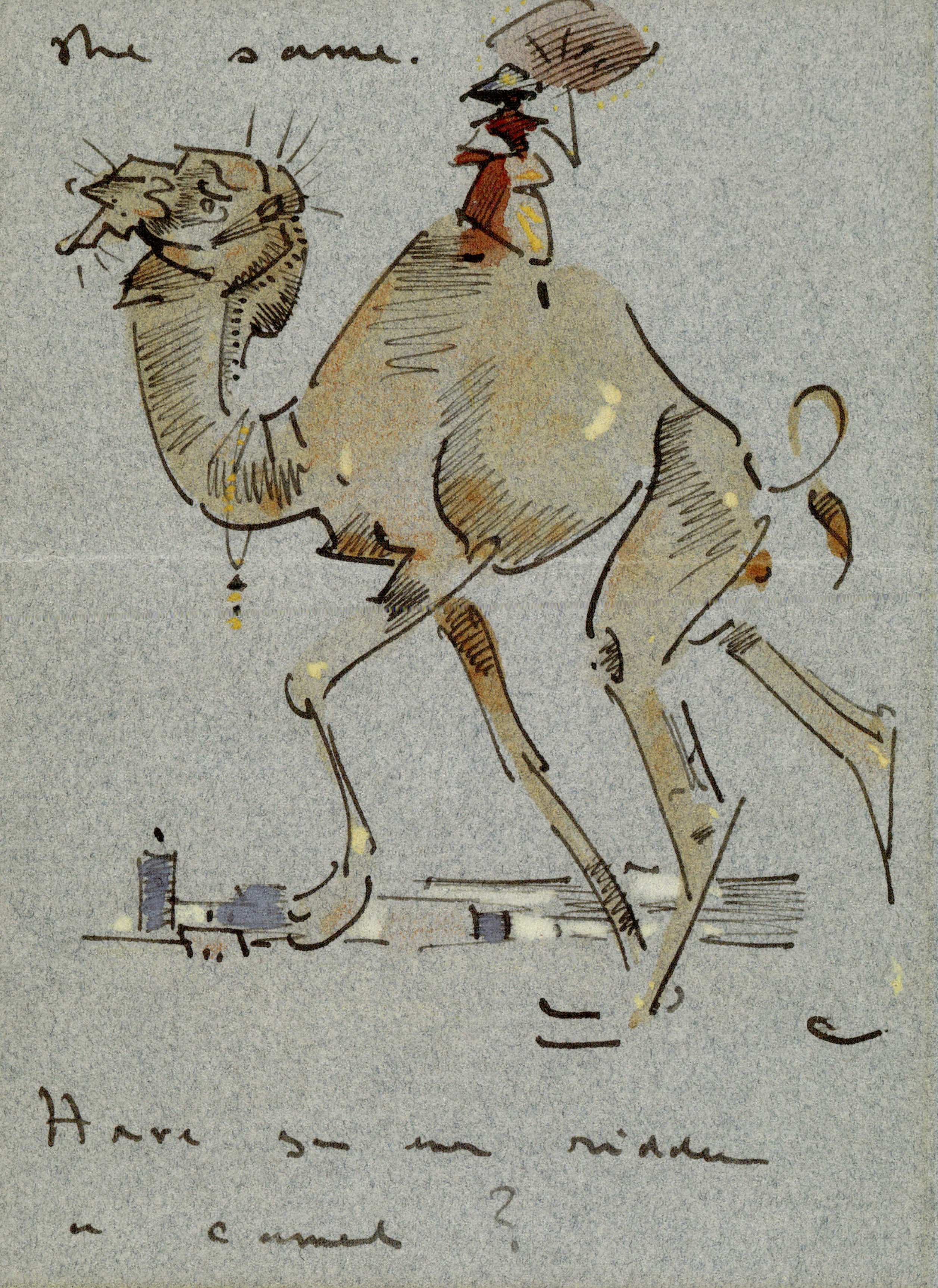
the same.
Have you ever ridden
a camel?

# Humour

Whether quick sketches for family and friends or more developed compositions, Crawhall's watercolours and drawings demonstrate a lively wit, a trait inherited from his father. A close friend of the illustrator Charles Keene, Crawhall's father regularly supplied him between 1877 and 1890 with material for publication in the satirical magazine *Punch*. Some of these cartoons make difficult viewing, revealing offensive racist and misogynistic attitudes. The same is true of a number of Crawhall's own drawings. His humour also reflects different cultural stances on hunting and animal performance to those of today. Additionally, as evident from his early drawing of a bull charging a fisherman (p. 8), in which he emphasized the bull's masculinity and stud credentials, Crawhall showed a tendency towards a rather bawdy humour. However, Crawhall's pictorial wit often revolved around more innocent and delightful juxtapositions of different creatures, comic pairings of people and animals and the peculiarities of observed animal behaviour.

Most notable among Crawhall's humorous drawings are those he made for Marie (Mary) Ida Frida Auras (1888–1956), a young German girl he met through Lavery around 1900. She travelled around Europe, North Africa and America with the Laverys, modelling for Lavery's paintings and acting as companion to his daughter Eileen (1890–1935). Crawhall wrote to her, amusing her with funny drawings of animals, entertaining incidents or imagined scenarios in which Auras was the heroine. In 1922 Burrell purchased 46 Crawhall drawings and illustrated letters from Auras, by then Mrs Black-Hawkins.

Opposite: ***Lady Riding a Camel,*** about 1902
Pen and wash on paper
15.7 x 11.5 cm
35.93

In this typically humorous drawing in a letter to his friend Mary Auras, Crawhall depicts her sedately perched on top of an enormous camel holding a parasol. He writes: 'Have you ever ridden a camel?'

Crawhall's humour appealed to Burrell, who was also a keen collector of the satirical drawings of English caricaturist Phil May (1864–1903), Crawhall's contemporary. Like May, Crawhall sometimes mocked the excesses and absurdities of modern life. They admired each other's work and Burrell delighted in both men's visual wit and elegant economy of line. Interestingly, May also loved horses and had at one time intended to become a jockey. Incredibly, he and Crawhall also looked like each other, shocking themselves at their personal resemblance when they first met at the Savage Club in London in the 1890s. However, whereas May was a flâneur, an observer of society, culture and fashion, Crawhall was an avid spectator of the animal kingdom and he reflected on modernity largely only as far as it impinged on the animal world.

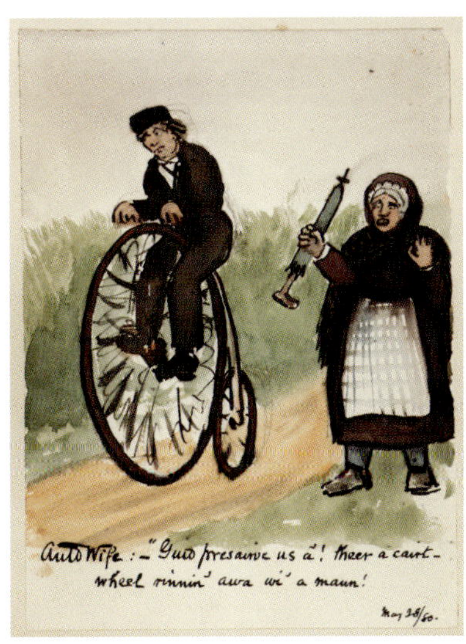


Crawhall's father drew many humorous sketches based on incidents that he observed, such as this encounter with a penny-farthing or high-wheeler bicycle, captioned 'Guid presairve us a'! Theer a cairt-wheel rinnin' awa wi' a maun!' Joseph Crawhall snr, 1800, ink on paper, vol. 12 of 21 albums of drawings submitted to Charles Keene for publication in *Punch*. Glasgow Museums, GML.2021.1.9.v.

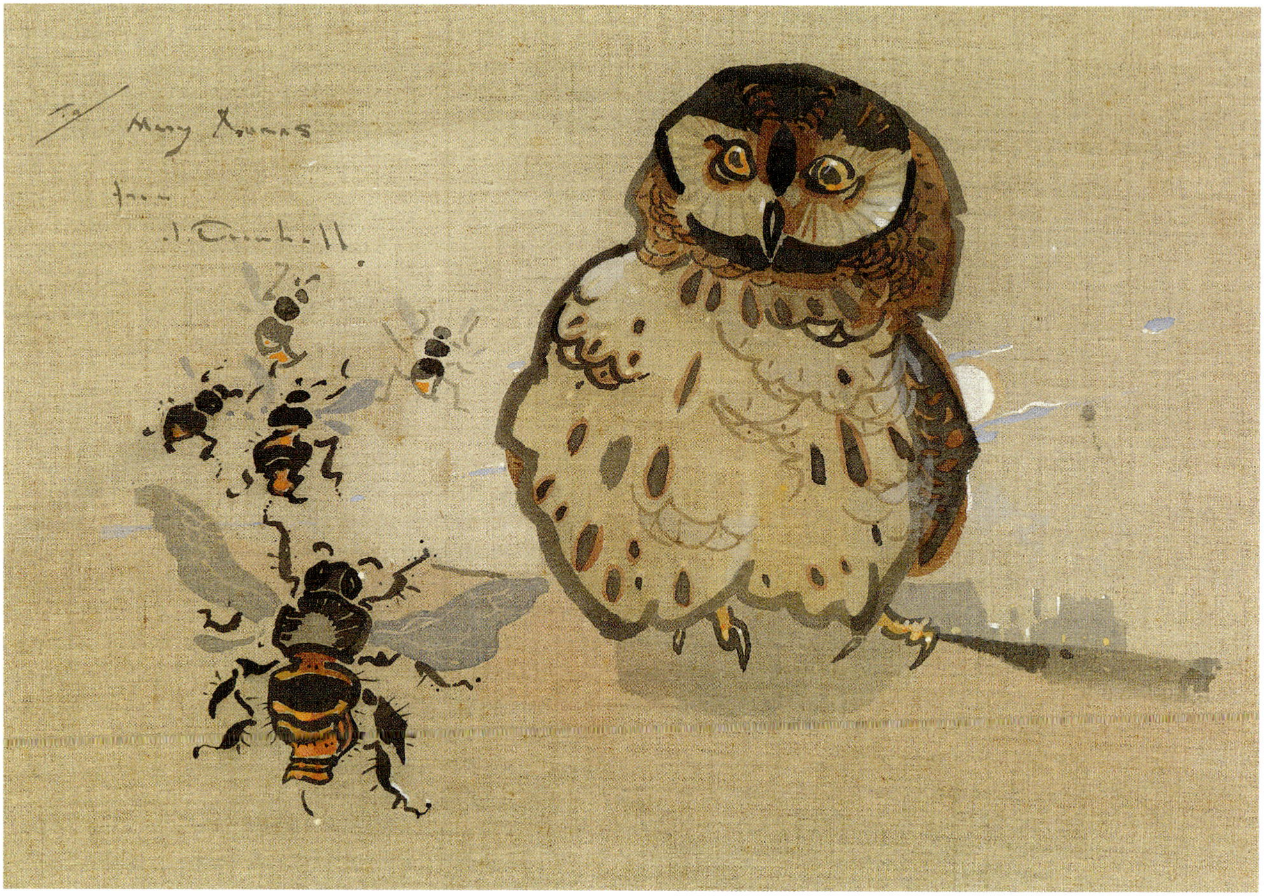

***Owl and Bees,*** about 1900–04
Watercolour and bodycolour on linen
24.2 x 33.1 cm
Inscribed 'To / Mary AURAS / from / J. Crawhall.'
35.169

A playful image, this watercolour shows a
confrontation between an owl and a contingent of
bees. Crawhall contrasts the round feathery shape
of the bemused owl with the hostile angularity of the
bees. It is more finished than many of the quickly
sketched drawings Crawhall made for Auras. The
nocturnal setting may seem strange but possibly
derives from behaviour Crawhall witnessed as some
species of bee are active at night, while others can
become aggressive if disturbed after dark. Owl nests
are frequently taken over by bee colonies. Or could
the inspiration have come from his father?

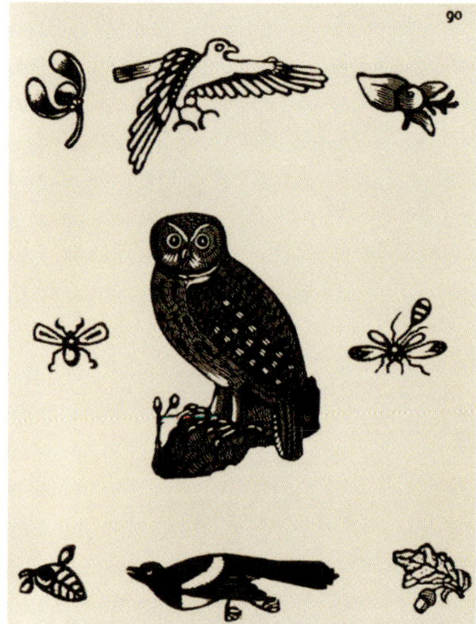

This page of
individual woodcut
designs by
Crawhall's father
comes from a
volume that brings
together illustrations
from several of his
publications. Here
an owl is grouped
with various flying
insects to humorous
effect. Joseph
Crawhall snr, from
*Impresses Quaint*,
1889. Glasgow
Museums Archive,
GMA.2013.1.6.850.

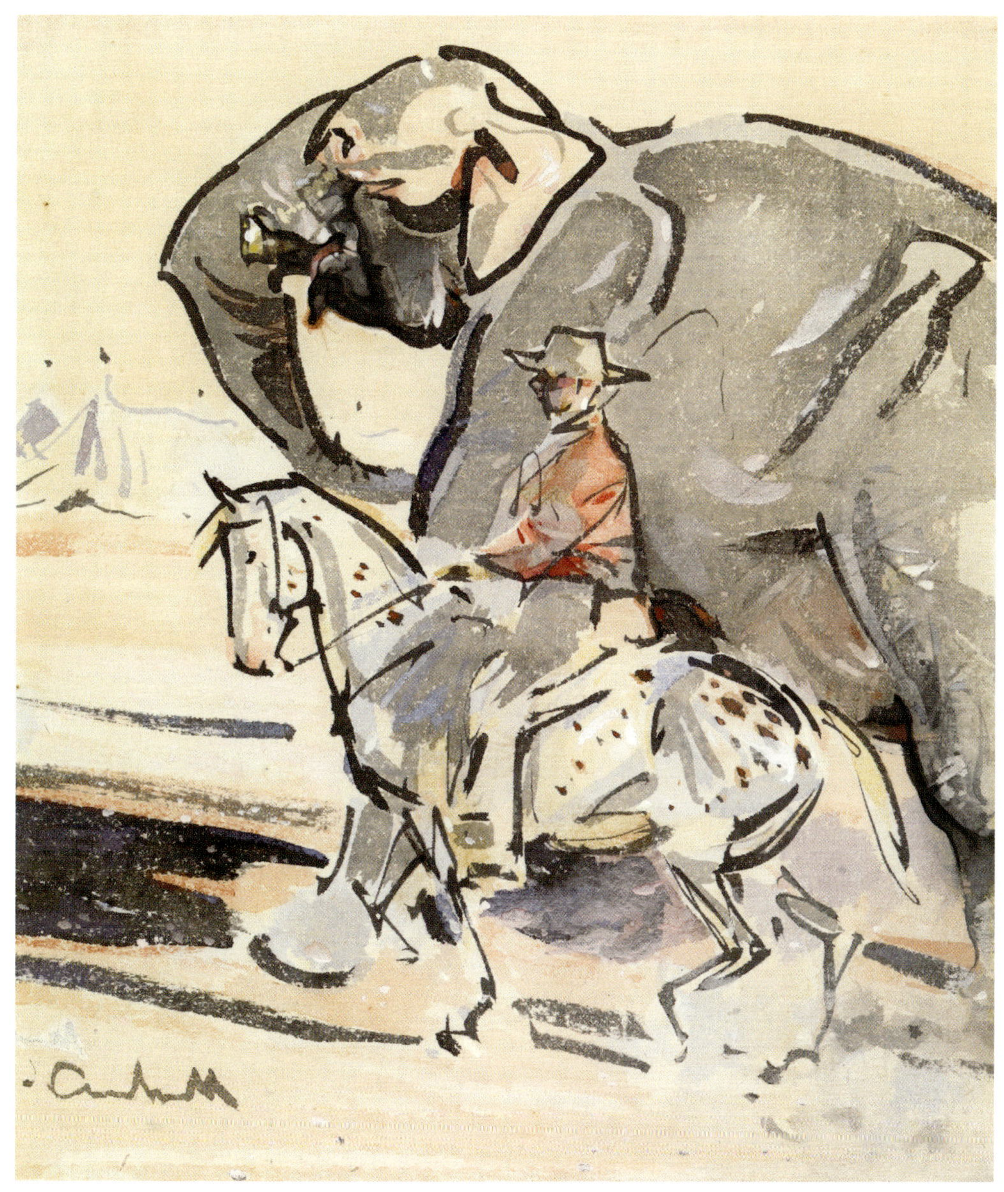

***Elephant and Circus Pony,*** about 1894–98
Bodycolour on linen
33 x 27.4 cm
35.111

Elephants were a major feature of circuses in the nineteenth century, often taught to do tricks and minor acrobatics. This drawing was probably based on a show that Crawhall witnessed. The comedy comes from the contrast of forms and gaits as the large ungainly elephant and elegantly collected Appaloosa horse are set around the ring. However, the whip carried by the man on horseback is a reminder of the fear of punishment that lay behind many animal acts. Crawhall's friend Cunninghame Graham described such performances as a 'cruel spectacle', stating that 'elephants were not intended to be clowns'.

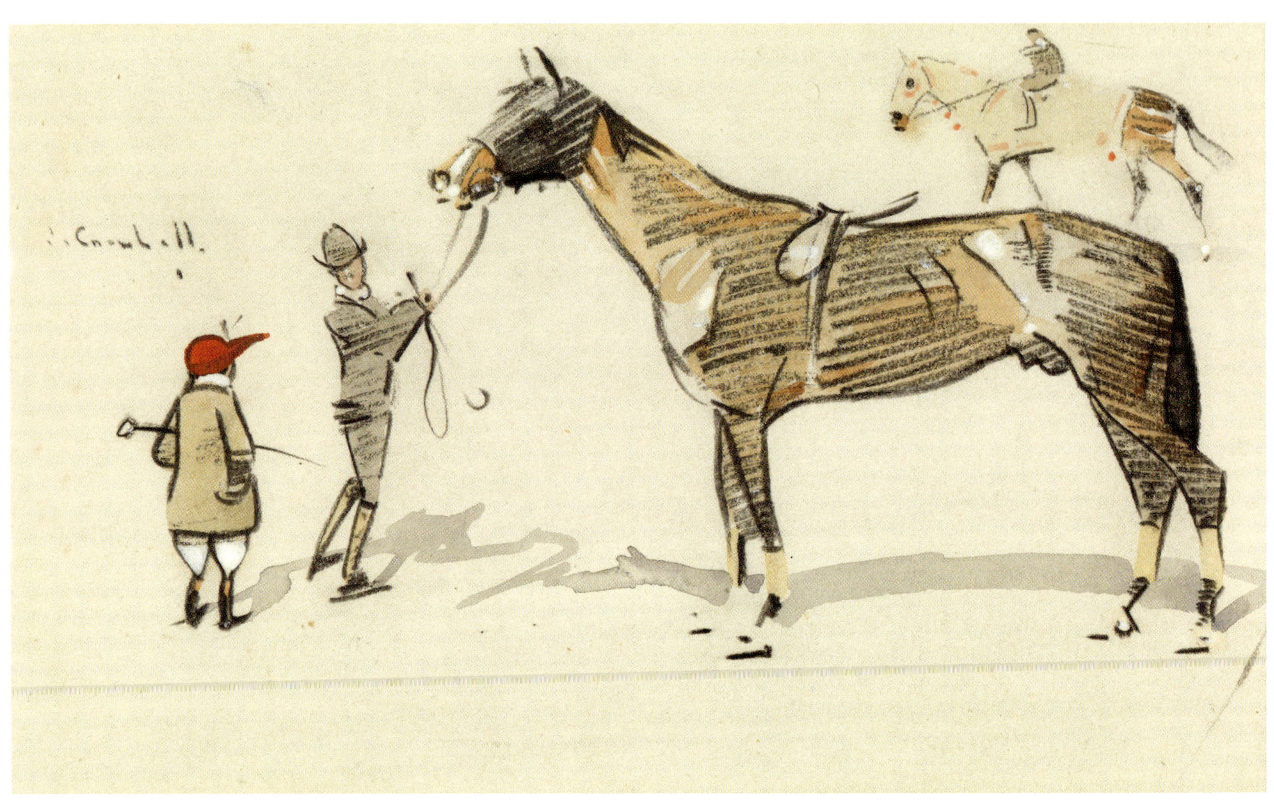


**_Racehorse and Jockey,_** possibly early 1900s
Chalk, graphite pencil and wash on paper
18.4 x 24.5 cm
35.181

In this drawing Crawhall beautifully captures the grace and nobility of the racehorse with its alert ears, long neck, fine limbs and elegant posture. He pointedly contrasts the animal with the squat figure of the jockey, made comic in his red cap with its exaggerated peak, oversized whip, flared white jodhpurs and tiny legs. More bestial than the horse, the jockey absent-mindedly scratches himself. The racehorse's hood, commonly used for highly-strung animals, portents danger, bringing to mind the anonymity of an executioner. The racetrack provided much scope for witty commentary for Crawhall, who often focused on disparities between refined horse and inept rider.

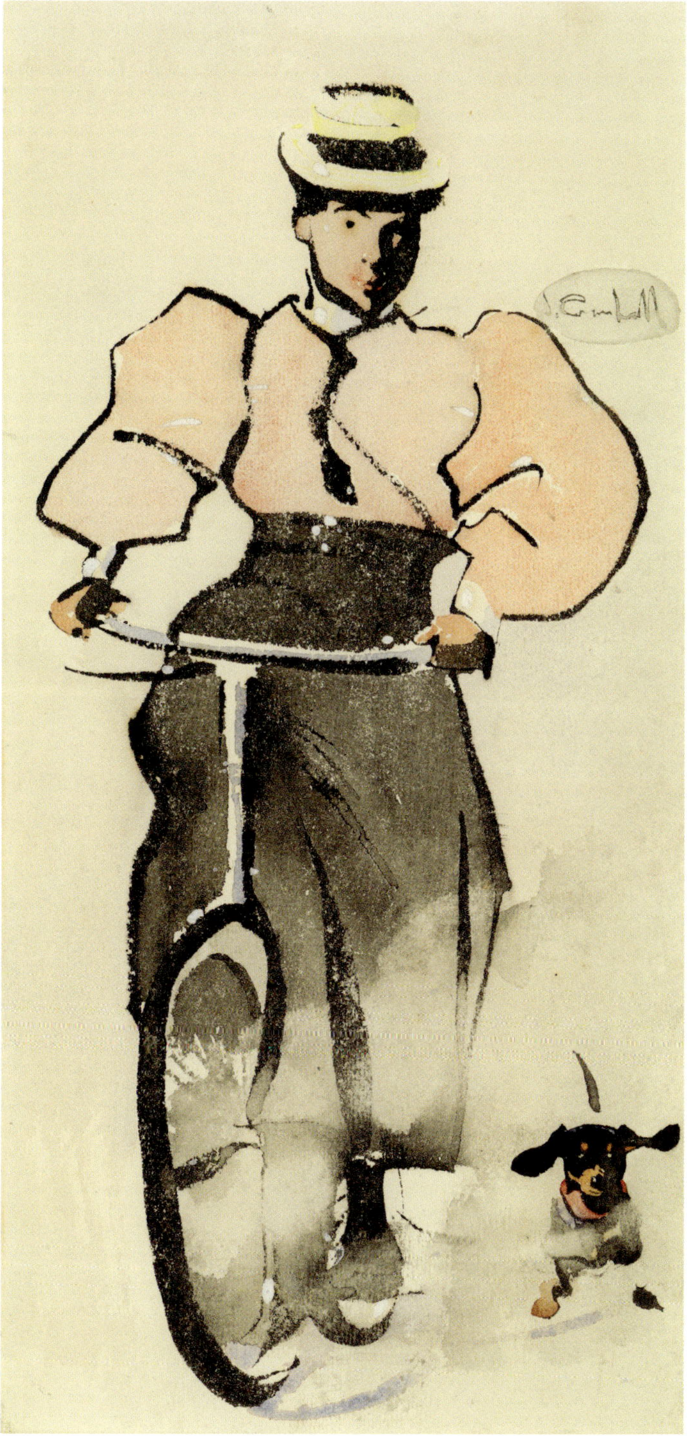

***Girl on a Bicycle,*** about 1896
Watercolour with wash and bodycolour
on paper
28.7 x 13.4 cm
35.124

This work is a striking symbol of modernity.
Cycling had become a popular pursuit
among urban women with the invention
of the safety bicycle. Fashions changed to
accommodate riding, with shorter more
practical skirts and even bloomers worn.
Bringing women greater freedom and
independence, cycling became associated
with the 'New Woman' and the suffrage
struggle for equal rights.

However, showing his sister Beatrice in the
saddle with the family dachshund Fritz in hot
pursuit, ears comically flapping, paint blurred
around bicycle spokes and dog legs to
suggest speed, Crawhall's watercolour was
no doubt intended to be humorous.

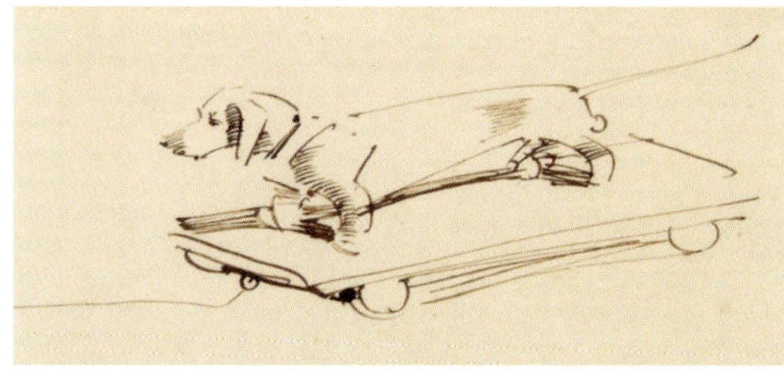

The short legs and slow pace of Fritz the dog was
obviously a Crawhall family joke, as evident from this
sketch in which he is provided with wheels. *Fritz on
a Trolley*, 1890s, by Joseph Crawhall, pen and ink on
paper. Glasgow Museums, PR.1943.8.2.

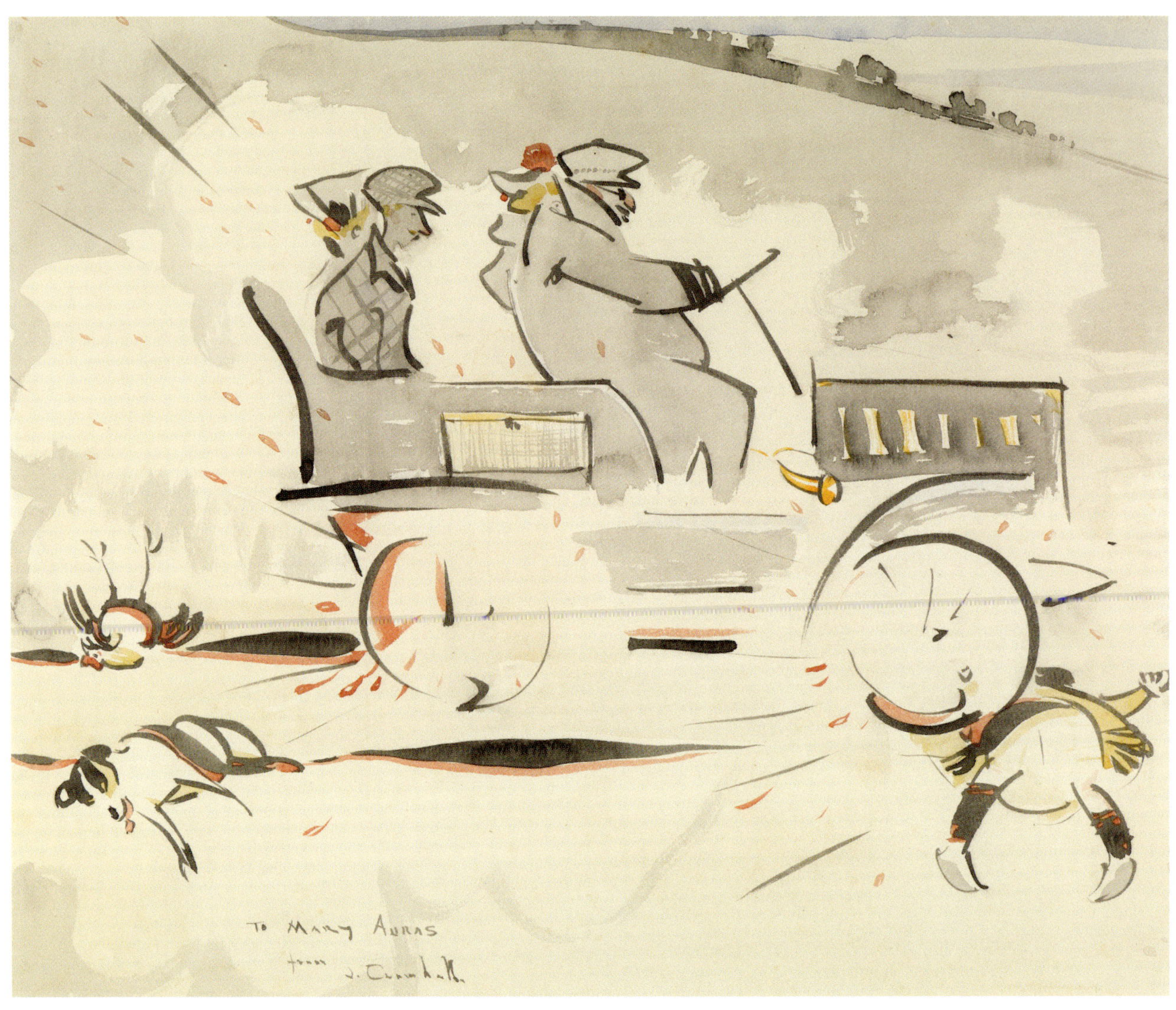


### *The Road Hog,* about 1900–04
Wash on paper
36 x 42 cm
Inscribed and signed lower edge 'To MARY AURAS /
from / J. Crawhall.'
35.185

The automobile was invented in Germany in 1885.
By the late 1890s they were being driven in Britain,
bringing immense changes to a society which had previously relied on horses and bicycles for
transportation by road. Crawhall's view of the motor
car and the kind of people who drove them is
expressed in this satirical drawing for Auras. A dog,
chicken and man in a kilt have all gone under its
wheels, its black tyres marking their bodies, blood
splattering in its wake. The four people inside the
vehicle with hats on and collars up, seem oblivious
to the carnage around them.

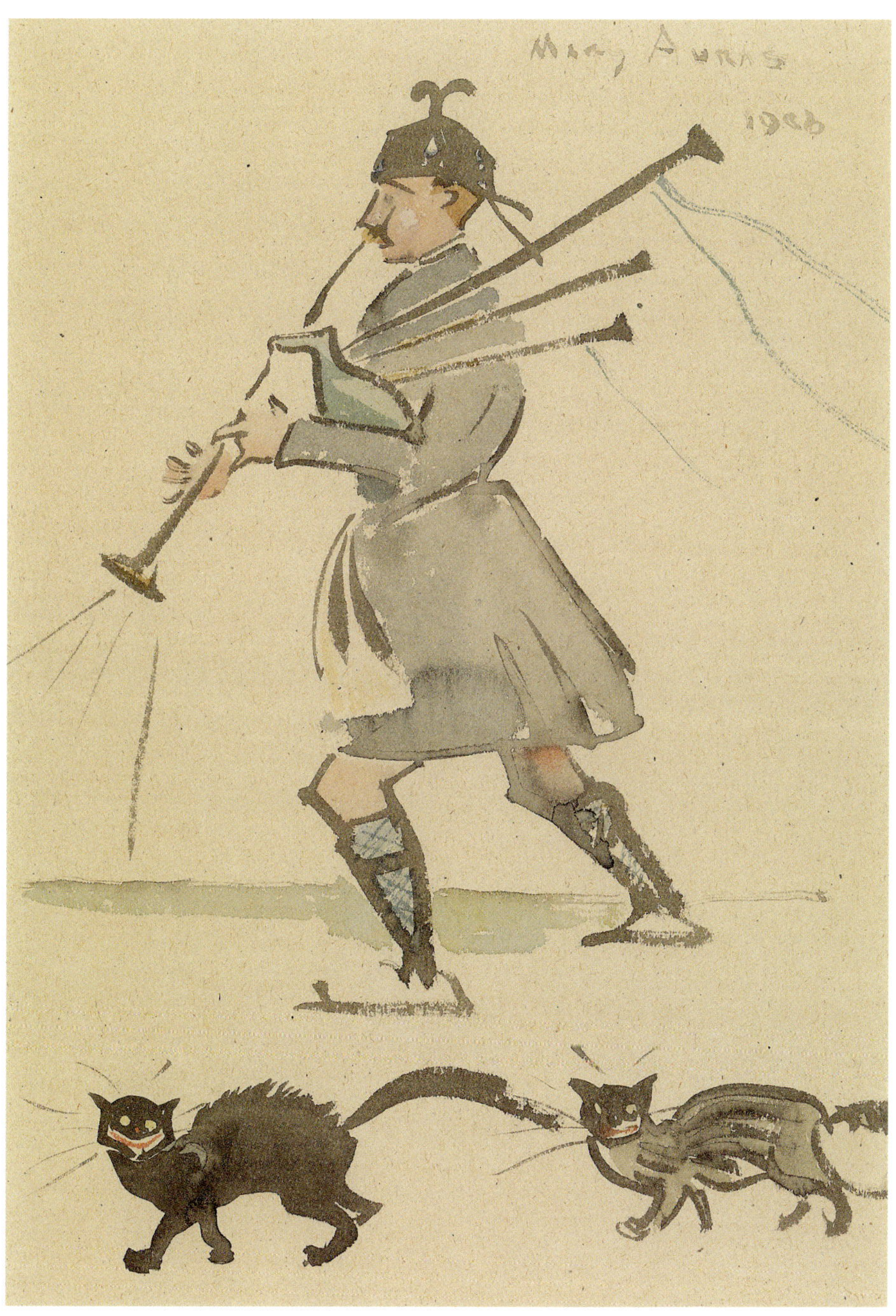


**Highlander Playing Bagpipes,** 1901
Wash on paper
37.9 x 25.0 cm
Inscribed upper right
'MARY AURAS / 1900'
35.134

This drawing of cats in stride with a bagpiper, grinning and yowling in accompaniment, was another mischievous drawing for Auras. The piper's feathered cap and bagpipe ribbons playfully mirror the cats' ears and whiskers. The occasion for Crawhall's joke may have been a trip to Scotland, an allusion to his friendship with the Glasgow Boys or an entertaining reference to his mother's Scottish ancestry. It may also have been a response to his father's humour and musical tastes, shared with Keene, an avid bagpipe collector and performer – bagpipers often appeared in Crawhall's father's comical drawings. However, the date, overwritten by Crawhall changing 1900 to 1901, would perhaps indicate a New Year's celebration.

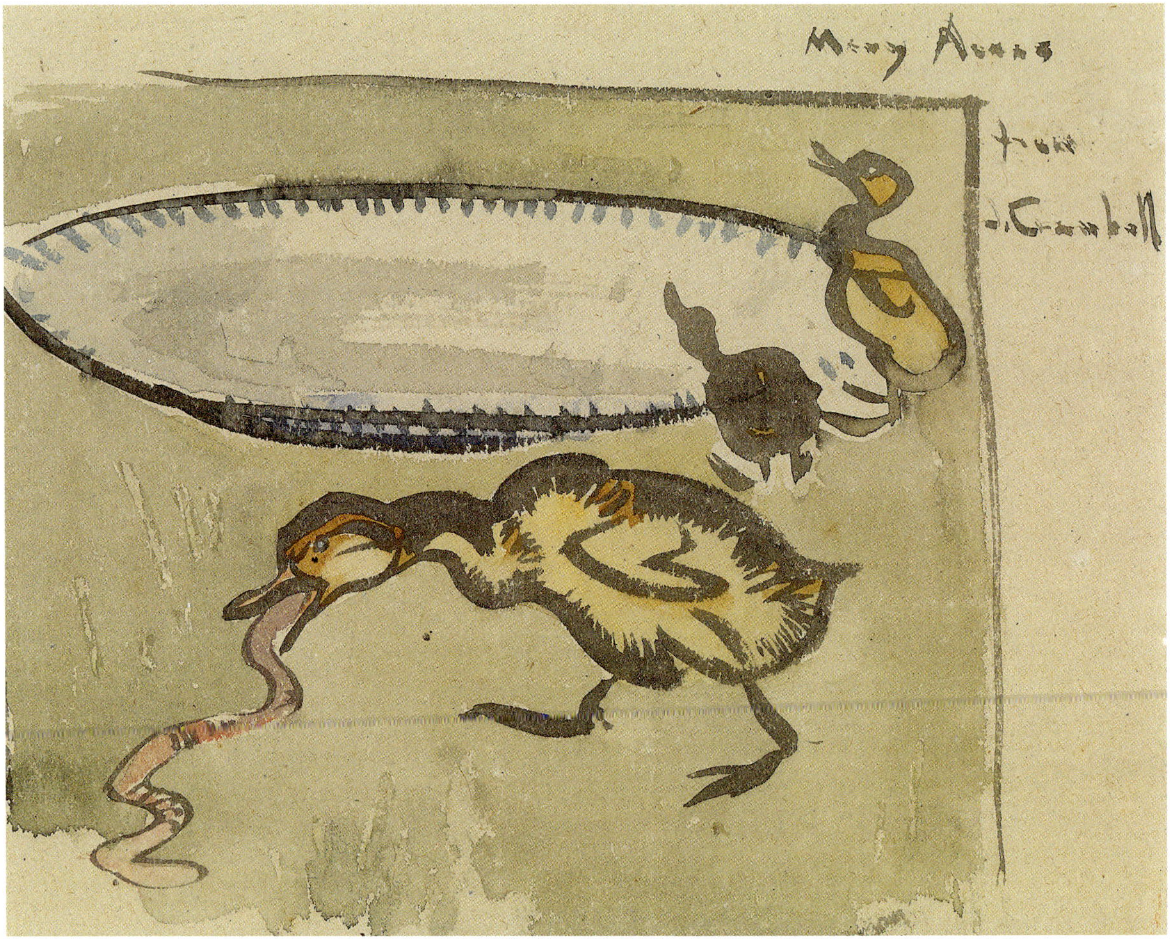
Merry Xmas
from
J. Crawhall

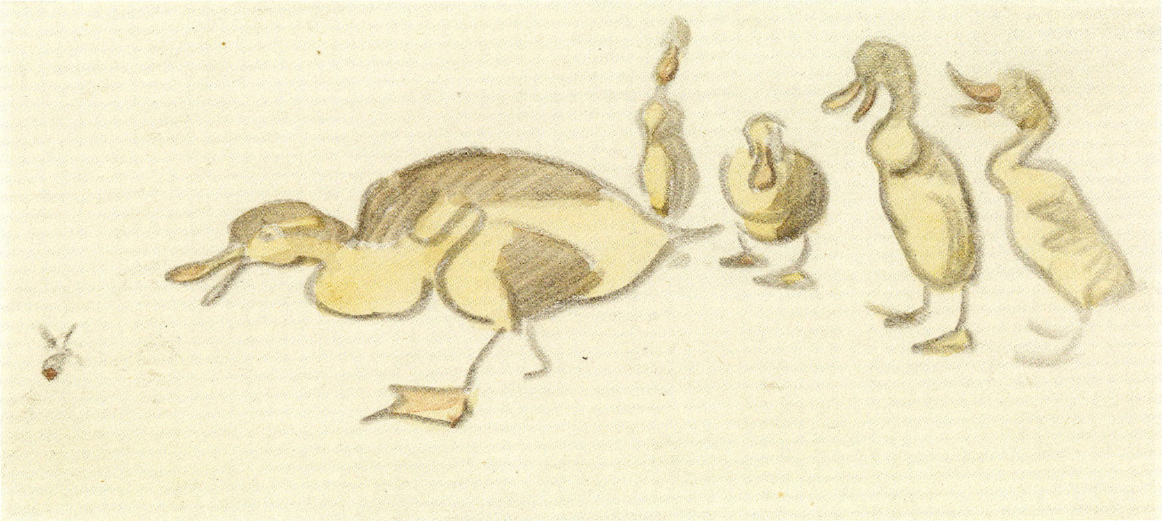

Left upper: ***Ducks and Worm,***
about 1900–04
Wash on paper
20.6 x 24.5 cm
Inscribed and signed upper right
'MARY AURAS from J. Crawhall'
35.108

Left lower: ***Ducks and Insect,***
about 1900–04
Graphite pencil and wash on paper
8.4 x 17.4 cm
35.107

Right: ***Cold Chicken,***
about 1900–04
Wash on paper
20.5 x 11 cm
35.101

The inherent adorability of ducks and ducklings made them a favourite subject with Crawhall and Auras. In *Ducks and Insect*, each bird is given its own comic stance as they interact with the flying insect. The plucky duckling trying to swallow a large earthworm in *Ducks and Worm* is particularly funny. One can imagine the caption: 'Bitten off more than you can chew?' We do not know how pertinent these drawings were to actual circumstances. Could they have been entertaining comments on particular situations? Was *Cold Chicken*, which is typical of Crawhall's love of visual puns, a response to a complaint from Auras about an unappetizing dinner menu? However, sketches like *Ducks and Worm* and *Ducks and Insect* could equally have been simple light-hearted fun, based on observed or imagined incidents, summing up the comically determined and audacious nature of the duckling and the conviviality of duck community.

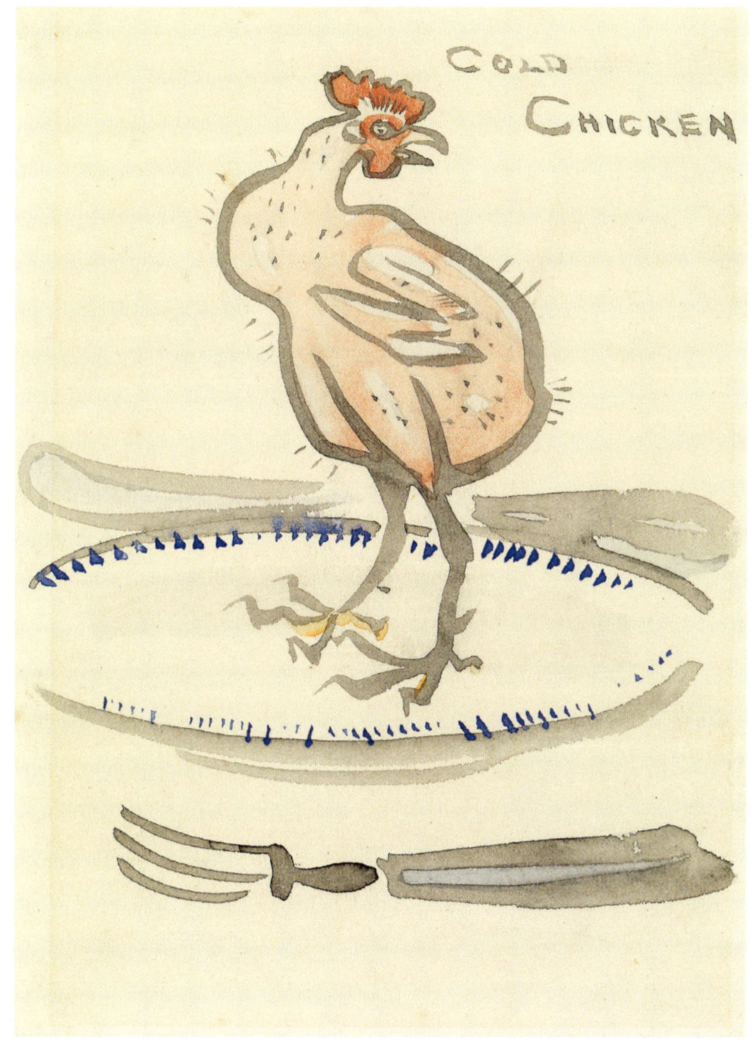

# Epilogue

In 1912 WB Paterson held a retrospective exhibition of Crawhall's work in his London gallery. The following year Crawhall died during a trip to London to sell artworks, aged only 52, having suffered from lung problems throughout his life.

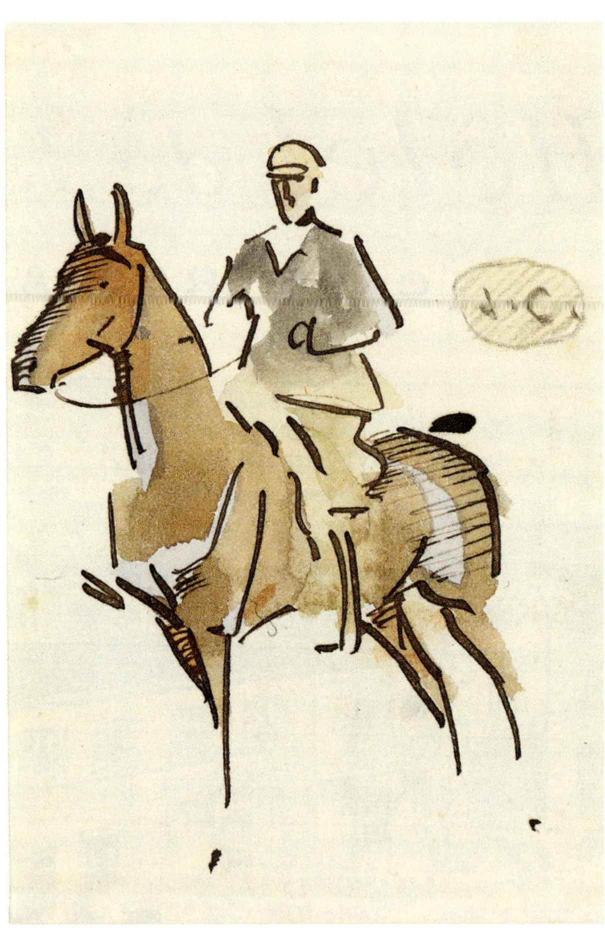

**Crawhall on Horseback,** about 1900–04
Pen, ink and wash on paper
9 x 6 cm
35.103

# Further Reading

Martin Bellamy and Isobel MacDonald, *William Burrell: A Collector's Life*, Glasgow Museums and Birlinn, Edinburgh, 2022. Biography of William Burrell, his life, collection and legacy.

George Denholm Armour, *Bridle and Brush: Reminiscences of an Artist Sportsman*, Eyre & Spottiswoode, London, 1937. Autobiography containing memories of Crawhall in Tangier and running a stud together in Hertfordshire.

Roger Billcliffe, *The Glasgow Boys*, Frances Lincoln, London, 1985, revised 2008. In-depth examination of the Glasgow Boys.

Roger Billcliffe, Kenneth McConkey, Mark O'Neill, Hugh Stevenson and Jean Walsh, *Pioneering Painters: The Glasgow Boys*, Glasgow Museums, 2010. Exhibition catalogue. Accessible introduction to the Glasgow Boys.

RB Cunninghame Graham, *Writ in Sand*, William Heinemann, London, 1932. Autobiographical memories of Tangier with Crawhall.

Frances Fowle, *Van Gogh's Twin: The Scottish Art Dealer Alexander Reid*, National Galleries of Scotland, Edinburgh, 2010. Biography of Reid discussing his relationship with Crawhall and the Glasgow Boys.

Vivien Hamilton, *Joseph Crawhall (1861–1913): One of the Glasgow Boys*, John Murray in association with Glasgow Museums, London, 1990. Key study of Crawhall, his life and art.

John Lavery, *The Life of a Painter*, Cassell & Co., London, 1940. Autobiography with memories of Crawhall, the Glasgow Boys and Tangier.

Kenneth McConkey, *John Lavery: A Painter and his World*, Atelier, Edinburgh, rev. ed. 2010. Detailed monograph on Lavery.